Shockinį   ⌐y
Deaths and Murders
Volume 2

Dylan Frost

Contents

94 - Rock Hudson
97 - David Huffman
98 - Steve Irwin
100 - Martin Luther King, Jr
101 - Sonny Liston
104 - Danny Lockin
106 - Jayne Mansfield
108 - Jenny Maxwell
109 - Freddie Mills
112 - Ashleigh Aston Moore
114 - Tommy Morrison
118 - Enriqueta Martí
119 - Benito Mussolini
121 - Dennis Nilsen
128 - Amanda Peterson
130 - Brad Renfro
131 - Natasha Richardson
134 - Boris Sagal
135 - Rod Serling
138 - Harold Shipman
140 - Paul Walker
142 - Shane Warne
143 - Jack Wild
145 - Aileen Wuornos
147 - Paula Yates

Introduction

A second all new volume of celebrity deaths and murders. The cases that follow are eclectic and darkly fascinating. Drug overdoses, murders, television suicides, crazed fans, unsolved deaths, autoerotic asphyxiation, car crashes, freak accidents, doomed child stars, and so on. New additions include James Dean, Peaches Geldof, Paul Walker, Steve Irwin, Whitney Houston, Christine Chubbuck, Lana Clarkson, Caroline Flack, Jayne Mansfield, and many more.

AL ADAMSON

Al Adamson was born on July the 25th, 1929, in Hollywood, California. He was a writer/producer/director of cheap but cheerful exploitation films in the 1960s and 1970s. He was responsible for strange cultish obscurities like Psycho A Go-Go (later worked into Blood of Ghastly Horror), Satan's Sadists, Horror of the Blood Monsters, Dracula Vs. Frankenstein (which was clearly ahead of its time given that films like Freddy Vs. Jason and Alien v Predator came decades later!), and Five Bloody Graves.

Adamson's film career was a long way from mainstream Hollywood and strictly bargain basement but he was never short of a few marketing gimmicks. His 1978 film Death Dimension (a.k.a. Freeze Bomb) featured no less than two former James Bond franchise stars in George Lazenby and Harold Sakata. Adamson also directed two kung fu films featuring Enter the Dragon star Jim Kelly. Adamson's 1983 film Lost featured the last ever performance by Sandra Dee.

The grade Z drive-in pictures of Adamson featured biker chicks, gore, nudity, and low-budget fun for those with a sweet tooth for trashy tongue-in-cheek schlock, car chases, explosions, action, kung fu, and horror. Adamson was described by some as something akin to a modern day Ed Wood. Sometimes he would even get the rights to an existing picture (like a western for example) and throw in a load of new scenes chock full of gore and sex. Adamson was never going to win an Oscar but he was inventive and very hard-working and his films were entertaining enough taken on their own terms. He also made uncredited appearances in many of his movies.

Adamson even filmed some of his movies at the ranch where the Charlie Manson cult lived. He also made some softcore erotic films in the 1970s to make ends meet and bring in some extra cash. You could probably describe Adamson as a grindhouse legend of sorts. The decline of the drive-in market probably affected Adamson's stock-in-trade and by the 1990s he was more or less retired. By now he was in his sixties and divided his time between his homes in California and Nevada. Adamson wasn't super rich but he had a modest nest egg and two homes so he wasn't doing too badly all things considered.

Somewhat vulnerable and lonely from the recent death of his wife (and frequent leading lady) Regina Carro, Adamson became friendly with a 50-year-old builder named Fred Fulford. Fulford became a live in contractor helping out with renovations at the house Adamson had in California. Though he had no way of knowing it, Adamson's decision to hire Fulford as a contractor would cost him his life. Fulford would be responsible for Adamson's macabre death - the director meeting a fate rather akin to a character in one of his films.

Adamson was by all accounts an affable and decent person and didn't deserve what fate had in store for him.

In 1995, Adamson was reported missing by his brother and friends after they didn't see him for weeks. This was all very suspicious and unusual as far as they were concerned. It was very out of character for Al to suddenly go away without telling anyone. His brother felt sure that Al wouldn't have gone on a vacation or trip without informing him first so he naturally became worried. The chief suspect in Al's disappearance was obviously going to be a certain Fred Fulford. Fulford had spent a lot of time with Al lately and more or less lived at the house. If anyone knew what had happened to Al it was surely going to be Fred Fulford.

When it transpired that Fulford had gone away too this case suddenly became even more suspicious. Eventually it was decided to search Al's home for signs of any clues that might potentially explain what had happened to him and why he had apparently vanished without trace. It was during this search that a grisly and tragic discovery was made. The 66 year-old Adamson was found dead and buried in cement where a jacuzzi had been. No prizes for guessing who the prime suspect in this case was now. It was probably not going to take a genius lawyer to convict Fulford.

Fred Fulford was (no surprise here) later tried and convicted of the murder of Al Adamson. Deputy District Attorney Paul Vinegrad maintained, based on pathology results, that Fulford had bashed in Adamson's skull with a blunt heavy object and then dumped his body in the jacuzzi pit and poured a huge amount of cement over the crime scene. "This really is an overwhelming case of guilt," Vinegrad said. Given that Fulford was being employed to make renovations to the home he must have had plenty of cement on hand for this ghastly attempt to hid Al's body.

The court case established that Adamson and Fulford had a financial agreement. They were going to sell the house after Fulford had completed all the repairs and renovations and then split the money from the sale of the property. It appears then that there was some sort of disagreement or money related argument which made Fulford blow a fuse and kill Adamson. After the murder, Fulford had fled to Florida. He was even brazen enough to have Adamson's cars shipped over - whereupon he sold them.

Fulford preposterously claimed at the trial that he had no idea Adamson had been murdered and had assumed his employer's disappearance was due to the fact that Al had taken a vacation. Fulford then claimed that he had been framed for the murder but this was patently a desperate untruth. Fulford's unconvincing and fantastical pleas of innocence, predictably, did not stand up to much scrutiny in court and he was sentenced to a 25-years-to-life term in prison in 2000. There was a lengthy delay in getting an actual trial on this case because it took some time to extradite Fulford from Florida.

Fred Fulford has come up for parole a few times but the parole board has so far denied his request to be released. Adamson, a kind and well liked character, had clearly made a terrible error of judgment when he became friends with Fulford and entered into a business arrangement with him. Perhaps Fulford, clearly a disturbed and dangerous individual, hid his dark side well. The end result was tragic.

One darkly ironic thing about this case is that, before his death, Adamson had planned to return to filmmaking and even had an unproduced horror script about a man who is murdered and buried in his own house over a financial dispute. In 2020 it was announced that a special box-set featuring many of Al Adamson's old films would be released. It's just a shame that Al didn't live to see this happen.

GWILI ANDRE

Gwili Andre was born Guri Anderson on February the 4th, 1908 in Copenhagen, Denmark. Andre became a famous model in Europe and graced many magazine covers. While many people lived on the breadline in those dark days she earned $25,000 a year during the Depression and was much in demand. Her potential seemed unlimited. Gwili then moved to the United States where her statuesque blonde good looks earned her a film contract with RKO. In those days (and maybe it hasn't changed so much even now) studios would discover an attractive young woman and then try to mould her into an actress. While this sometimes worked surprisingly well there are plenty of failures too. When it came to Hollywood, Gwili Andre was destined to become what you might describe as a failed experiment.

Andre was compared to Garbo and Marlene Dietrich and featured in many gossip and entertainment articles. At one point she is alleged to have dated Howard Hughes. The stars seemed to have aligned for Gwili Andre and she was tipped to become a huge movie star. There was only one small problem. Gwili Andre couldn't act to save her life. Her early films roles were pre-code movies Roar of the Dragon, Secrets of the French Police, and No Other Woman. Andre certainly looked the part of a film star but there was something missing. She lacked the screen presence and natural relaxed charisma and wit of the great Hollywood female actors. She made the dialogue sound flat. Gwili Andre always looked and sounded like she was reading her lines off cue cards.

Critics were harsh on Gwili Andre's acting talents and described her performances as lifeless and wooden. The columnist Frank Morris would later write - 'I have to think hard to recall the names of any of the other actresses who were foisted on the screen as Greta Garbo imitators. One of them, nevertheless, was Gwili Andre. Miss Andre was a fashion model, and she photographed to perfection. As her studio groomed her for stardom, the fan magazines and the newspapers blossomed with pictures of her. There was a more than ordinary interest in Miss Andre. Alas, in her first picture she proved to be such a stiff, colorless and completely talentless performer that she disappeared almost overnight.'

With her Hollywood career stuck in neutral and going nowhere fast, Andre concentrated on being a model and took a break from films. She also got married during this period and had a son. Gwili Andre would only make two more films in the end. Her last credit was a supporting role in the 1942 crime drama The Falcon's Brother. She hadn't got any better when it came to the mysterious craft of thesping. Gwili still delivered her dialogue in a robotic and disinterested fashion and clearly did not have the acting chops to be anything other than a minor background player. This realisation must have been tough for Andre to cope with given the fact that she had been groomed for Hollywood stardom.

By now her window of opportunity when it came to movies had all but shut. Her limited acting ability meant that Hollywood had more or less washed its hands of Gwili Andre and moved onto new stars. There were no shortage of new beautiful blondes in Hollywood who aspired to be an actress so Gwili Andre became yesterday's news. Andre moved back to Denmark at one point and also got divorced. She is said to have become an alcoholic. In the end she decided to go back to the United States. She lived in New York at first but then (inevitably perhaps) made her way to California. Gwili Andre still had dreams of becoming a film star in Hollywood but these dreams were now unrealistic. Gwili was like a washed up boxer who still deludes himself that he could get his old title back.

On February the 5th, 1959, Gwili Andre died in a fire at her Venice Beach home. She was 52. The legend goes that, in a bizarre suicide ritual, she was found sprawled on the bedroom floor of her apartment, burned to a crisp in a funeral pyre she had made out of her old publicity clippings. After years of desperately trying to resurrect her career Gwili Andre had given up and allegedly taken her life in a most theatrical fashion. Whether or not this story is true or an urban myth is open to question. Investigators and neighbours found a scrapbook Gwili Andre had kept of her career as a model actually survived the flames. It seems apparent though that she was always wistful about the fact that she never quite managed to become a movie star. Her ashes were later buried at Søndermark Cemetery in Copenhagen.

PETER ARNE

Peter Arne was an English actor who was born in British Malaya (Malaysia). Although he never become tremendously famous, Arne was one of those actors where you'd probably recognise his face even if you didn't know what his name was. He settled in Britain after serving in the RAF during the war. After establishing himself on the stage he became a prolific film and television actor. Arne would often play shifty crisp sounding villains or suave foreign characters. In the 1960s he appeared in popular TV shows like Danger Man, The Saint, The Champions and The Avengers. In 1968 he played Captain of Bomburst in the children's film Chitty Chitty Bang Bang and also had a role in Khartoum. His other film roles included The Cockleshell Heroes and Ice Cold in Alex. Arne was all over the place. You've probably watched him in dozens of things without ever knowing what his name was in real life.

In the next decade Arne appeared in many more films - including Straw Dogs, The Return of the Pink Panther, Agatha, and When Eight Bells Toll. Despite appearing in big movies, Arne was always more of a background actor and more than willing to supplement his income with television work. He even took a part in the infamously bad soap opera Triangle. Triangle was a BBC soap set aboard a North Sea ferry that sailed from Felixstowe to Gothenburg and Gothenburg to Amsterdam. The show was openly mocked by critics but actually ran for three seasons. Trivia you'll never need - one of the regulars in Triangle was Jonathan Scott-Taylor. Scott-Taylor was the kid who played Damien Thorn in Damien: Omen II.

Despite his dalliance with Triangle, Peter Arne was still picking up plenty of film work in the 1980s though and appeared in Victor Victoria, Trail of the Pink Panther, and Curse of the Pink Panther - all for the director Blake Edwards. He was happy and content in real life too. Arne had a Knightsbridge flat near Harrods and a country house in Devon. He was popular socially and attended many parties. Arne was said to be a great storyteller so he was a popular party guest. He was gay but because he moved in theatrical circles this was never much of a problem for him.

On the 1st of August 1983, Arne, who had agreed to play a part in a forthcoming episode of Doctor Who, was sorting out his costume at the BBC studio. Later that day he went back to his flat where something very odd and tragic obviously happened. Arne was later found beaten to death in the hallway of his ground-floor flat. He was 62 years old. It was a violent death and must have been very shocking for his neighbours when they found out. The neighbours had earlier reported hearing a commotion and noises suggesting a struggle of some sort was taking in Arne's flat.

Peter Arne was bludgeoned to death with a log from his fire and also a stool. It was a brutal and deadly attack. Because there was no sign of any forced entry the police obviously deduced that Arne must have known the killer and willingly let the suspect into the flat. That deduction proved to be on the money. Peter Arne did indeed know the person who killed him. The main suspect was a homeless man who lived rough nearby. Arne obviously knew this man because he used to give him some food from time to time.

A few days later an Italian man named Giuseppe Perusi was found dead in the River Thames. His death was ruled a suicide. Perusi was the homeless man whom Arne had sometimes given some food to. The official verdict is that Perusi, for reasons best known to himself (or maybe due to the fact he was mentally unstable), had murdered Arne and then drowned himself. It could be that the two men argued over something. At the time the gossip in the tabloids was that Arne's sexuality may have been a factor in his death although what exactly they meant by that is open to question. It seemed a trifle distasteful to say the least to speculate in this way.

There is still though a certain degree of mystery surrounding the death of Peter Arne. We simply don't know what really happened on that fateful and tragic afternoon. Arne was a remarkably prolific and versatile sort of actor who never was never short of work. His strange and violent death was a tragic last act in his life. Who knows, if he hadn't been murdered, maybe Peter Arne would eventually have found a role that finally made him a household name.

ARTHUR ASHE

Arthur Ashe was born July 10, 1943, in Richmond, Virginia. Ashe began playing tennis at the age of seven and was the first black player selected to the United States Davis Cup team and the only black man ever to win the singles title at Wimbledon, the US Open, and the Australian Open. Ashe was truly a trailblazer. He was also an intelligent and sensitive man who elicited great admiration and respect in anyone who came into contact with him.

Ashe joined the United States Army on August 4, 1966. He completed his basic training in Washington and was later commissioned as a second lieutenant in the Adjutant General Corps. He was assigned to the United States Military Academy at West Point. He ran a tennis program while in the armed forces and then embarked on a remarkable career in the sport when he left. Ashe was a natural athlete and in tennis found something he was amazingly gifted in.

It was definitely not easy for Arthur Ashe on the tennis circuit in the early days. Tennis, at the time, was still seen as a rather white and snooty country club sort of game and there was plenty of ingrained prejudice. "Get the n***** off the court," one white patron infamously shouted in March 1969 while Ashe was practicing at a country club in St. Petersburg, Florida. This was the sort of stuff Arthur Ashe had to put up with as her carved out a remarkable tennis career. This was also the sort of stuff that the Williams sisters (Serena and Venus) later had to put up with too when they started. Their father Richard withdrew Venus and Serena from a tennis academy when they were youngsters because of the casual prejudice he had detected. Richard Williams coached them himself - with great success.

Tiger Woods also had similar experiences on his path to fame. The world of golf had never really experienced a black golfer becoming its main star and best player before. Tiger had to endure some unfortunate snobbery and casual racism on his path to superstardom. After winning the 1997 Masters Tournament, Woods had to put up with a silly comment from Fuzzy Zoeller, who won this championship in 1979. Zoeller responded to Tiger's win by stating - "That little boy is driving well and he's putting well. He's doing everything it takes to win. So you know what you guys do when he gets in here. You pat him on the back and say congratulations and enjoy it and tell him not serve fried chicken next year. Got it." Tiger has said that he experienced much snootiness and racism at gold clubs when he was making his way as a golfer.

Arthur Ashe used his fame as a tennis player to campaign for civil rights and social justice. In 1973, Ashe went to the apartheid state of South Africa (which Arthur Ashe was naturally a vocal critic of and helped to exclude from the Davis Cup in 1970) to play in the national tennis championship there. Black civil rights leaders and celebrities in the United States had urged Ashe not to go but Arthur believed that the sight of a free and successful black man playing tennis in competition with whites (and beating them too) would offer hope to black people in South Africa. The gamble of Arthur Ashe worked. He was an inspiration to all the black people in South Africa who saw him. Arthur Ashe showed them that anything was possible.

Ashe supported the founding of the Association of Tennis Professionals and went on to become its elected president in 1974. After retiring from playing in 1980, he became captain of the U.S. Davis Cup team - a position he held from 1981 to 1985. Ashe underwent heart bypass operations in 1979 and 1983 - a bad heart was something that, sadly, ran in the family. In April 1992 he revealed that he had become infected with the virus that causes AIDS, most likely through a tainted blood transfusion received during one of those heart operations. He spent the rest of his life campaigning to raise more awareness for the disease. "If I were to say, God, why me? about the bad things," said Arthur Ashe, "then I should have said, God, why me? about the good things that happened in my life."

Arthur Ashe passed away in 1993 at the age of 49. It was a great shock that this incredible man had been taken so early. He was a thoughtful, intelligent person who impressed all that came into contact with him. And he was a terrific tennis player too and someone who battled prejudice and snobbery to take his rightful place in the sporting history books. Donald Dell, a close friend of Arthur Ashe, said - "Arthur Ashe has a quiet exterior but underneath lies someone who is very forceful, always changing, ever different, always a leader. He believes in striving for excellence by example, not by what he says, but what he does."

WILLIAM BURKE

William Burke and William Hare were two men from the north of Ireland who became infamous for their macabre activities in Edinburgh in 1827 and 1828. These two men became close friends when they moved to Scotland to work on a canal. Burke abandoned his family when he left Ireland and lived in Scotland with his mistress Helen McDougal. Hare lived very close by and ran a boarding house with Margaret Laird. Hare and Laird were not officially married but most people presumed they were man and wife.

At the end of 1827, one of the residents of the boarding house died of old age and Burke and Hare came up with a ghoulish way to recoup the money the old man owed in rent. They took the body to Edinburgh University where anatomy lecturer Professor Robert Knox was more than happy to take it off their hands. At the time there were strict laws about using corpses for medical research and training. Medical schools and universities could only use the corpses of prisoners, street orphans, or suicides in such research. As a consequence of this there was a shortage of cadavers for medical students and professionals to train and teach with.

Professor Robert Knox paid Burke and Hare seven pounds for the corpse of the boarding resident and the two men quickly deduced they might have stumbled across a lucrative - if grim - new business idea. Early in the new year, another resident of the boarding began to show signs of illness and Burke and Hare took great interest because they anticipated having another corpse to sell to Knox. They weren't willing to wait and decided to hasten the poorly man's departure from this mortal coil by suffocating him. They chose this method of murder because it left the corpse undamaged. A corpse with no injuries was more highly prized by medical schools and universities.

After selling the corpse of this second man to the university, Burke and Hare were rather frustrated by the good health of other residents in the boarding house. They decided to take matters into their own hands and began luring people to the boarding house so that they could kill them and sell the body. The greed and ruthlessness of these men was apparent when they killed an elderly woman and her blind grandson. It is believed that Burke and Hare killed around sixteen people in all although the true figure is felt by most to have probably been higher than this. They received between seven and ten pounds for the corpses they sold to the university.

The two men got so greedy and desperate for corpses in the end they even killed a relative of Burke's mistress Helen McDougal. Street prostitutes were among their victims because these were easy targets and not always likely to be missed by anyone or even reported as missing. Problems arose for this wicked duo though when medical students at the university began to recognise some of the corpses they were using in their training and studies. These included a few prostitutes and also a children's entertainer named James Wilson. By this stage there was also friction between Burke and Hare. Burke began to suspect that Hare was not sharing the money fairly and maybe even killing people alone for extra profits. As a consequence of this he started taking in lodgers of his own to kill!

The last victim was Marjory Campbell Docherty. Her body was stored at Burke's house but it was discovered by other lodgers named James and Ann Gray. Helen McDougal tried to bribe the Grays into keeping silent but they declined this offer and went to the police. Burke and Hare, along with Helen and Margaret Laird, were all arrested. Amazingly, Hare was offered immunity to testify against Burke because the prosecution didn't feel they had a huge amount of evidence. This brought protests from the family of victim James Wilson. At the trial, Hare tried to give the impression that he'd had nothing to do with the murders and that William Burke was the driving force behind them.

Helen McDougal was released at the end of the trial while

Margaret Laird served a short prison sentence. These two women were despised by the public and had to slip into obscurity for their own safety. William Burke was hanged at Lawnmarket on the 28th of January 1929. The judge ordered that his body should be donated to medical science and publicly dissected. You might say the judge thought of this as cosmic karma. Burke's skeleton is now on display at Surgeon's Hall in Edinburgh. William Hare was released in February 1829. He fled to England and essentially vanished. Professor Robert Knox was rather disgraced by his association with Burke and Hare and was more or less drummed out of the university and the medical establishment in Scotland. He never spoke about the case and eventually opened a medical practice far away in London.

SUSAN CABOT

Susan Cabot was born Harriet Pearl Shapiro in 1927. In the forties and fifties she was a glamourous and busy actress and had a contract with Universal at one point. She was probably best known for making a number of Westerns and she appeared in movies with the likes of Rock Hudson, Tony Curtis, Charles Bronson and Humphrey Bogart. Dark-haired and elegant - not to mention amazingly photographic - Cabot was romantically linked to King Hussein of Jordan and seemed to be on course to be a big star. In the 1950s though her star began to wane and she slid inexorably down the Hollywood pecking order. That's the way it occasionally goes in the film industry. Sometimes you are hot one minute and yesterday's news the next. You go from rising star to has-been in the blink of an eye.

Cabot ending up making a number of low-budget films for Roger Corman - the most famous of which was The Wasp Woman. She didn't have much enthusiasm for life as a B movie star and yearned to go back to the stage so that she could be taken more seriously. In 1964, Cabot had a son named Timothy Roman. She was married twice but ended up a single mother. She did some potato chip commercials to make ends meet in this decade. Behind the scenes Susan Cabot was a deeply troubled woman. Her mother had ended up in a mental institution and Susan Cabot spent much of her childhood in foster homes. It was later revealed that she had suffered sexual abuse in some of these foster homes and this awful experience left her with lifelong mental scars which affected her stability.

Susan Cabot eventually became elusive looking after her son. Those who lived near her said she was a quiet woman who rarely spoke to anyone if she could help it. Many said that Susan was a recluse. She made a TV appearance in 1970 but for all intents and purposes she was retired. Her house was said to full of squalor, rotting food, and dirt (though some contend this detail was exaggerated in court). Cabot was clearly someone who could barely look after herself - let alone a child. Mother and son were said to be inseparable and were never seen apart. Neighbours later said that they thought Susan Cabot was a bit weird to say the least.

Cabot's son had dwarfism and it is said that she gave him dodgy drugs in a desperate (and futile) attempt to make him taller. These drugs may have affected Timothy's mental health. Susan Cabot herself was suicidal and very unstable by now. They lived in the Encino area of Los Angeles. In 1986, 23 year-old Timothy bludgeoned his 59 year-old mother to death with a dumbbell. Timothy told the police that a ninja had entered the house and knocked him out. When he woke up he found his mother dead. You didn't need to be Columbo to work out that this was not what really happened. It is rather unlikely that a deadly ninja would be employed to target a former B movie actress and her dwarf son!

At the actual trial, Timothy said that he had been awoken by his mother screaming and she had attacked him with a dumbbell and a scalpel. He had seized the dumbbell and hit her to protect himself. Then he'd made up the story about the ninja in a desperate attempt to disguise what really happened. No one could ever really deduce what exactly happened when

Susan Cabot died but it was apparent that mother and son had an increasingly obstreperous and unhinged relationship. Things obviously came to some crazy head the night that Susan died.

Susan Cabot was said to be increasingly paranoid and troubled by the time of her death. Her mood swings made her unpredictable and potentially violent. Timothy's evidence concerning his mother attacking him that night was given some degree of veracity by the fact that he had a bruise on his head and a cut on his arm when he first spoke to the police. Most people seemed to believe that he had been attacked by his mother on the fateful day in question.

There was no real appetite by anyone in the legal system to throw the full weight of the law at Timothy Roman and lock him away for murder. He was clearly an abused and troubled young man suffering from confusion and drugged up to his eyeballs. He was therefore charged with involuntary manslaughter and given three years probation. There was no evidence at all of premeditation in Susan Cabot's death and this as much as anything is what enabled her son to get off fairly lightly (in most circumstances battering your mother to death would send you to prison for a very LONG time but this was clearly not a normal case - in fact, it was a rather unfathomable case).

The leniency shown to Timothy Roman was the human thing to do. Timothy Roman's other relatives expressed relief and gratitude at the merciful way the legal system had treated Timothy. One salient factor in the mercy shown to Timothy Roman is that he spent over two years in custody awaiting trial. You could say then that he'd already served two years in prison ever before any verdict on his ultimate fate had been decided by a court.

This was just a very weird and strange case where no one could ever quite establish what really happened in that house leading up to Susan's death. As a consequence of this it would clearly have been wrong to treat Susan Cabot's son like a cold blooded murderer. A rather strange postscript to this tragic affair is that the court case established that even up to her death Susan Cabot still received $1,500 a month from her former flame King Hussein (the money obviously explained why Susan Cabot was able to support herself and pay the bills despite not working herself anymore). This led to (unavoidable) speculation that the king was Timothy's father and the money was essentially child support. As for Timothy Roman, he died in 2003 of heart failure.

LANA CLARKSON

Lana Clarkson was born in Long Beach, California in 1962. She was a fashion model and actress. Clarkson was best known for B-movie roles but she had a number of small or background roles in mainstream movies like Fast Times at Ridgemont High, Brainstorm, and My Favorite Year. She also appeared in popular TV shows like Knight Rider, Three's Company, and The A-Team. Clarkson also appeared in five Roger Corman movies. You could probably describe Lana as a B-list star when it came to films. As a model though she went all over the world for photoshoots and was very successful.

Because her stock in trade was to play young pin-up type blondes, Clarkson found that her acting work began to dry up somewhat as she neared her forties. There was an endless assembly line of magazine model blondes in Hollywood so Clarkson eventually found the phone no longer rang as often as it used to. The sort of 'eye candy' background parts that she used to get in mainstream TV shows and movies were now being snapped up by younger women.

Ageism is a common complaint in Hollywood but it only seems to apply to women. Men can lead movies and get big paydays into their fifties and sixties but it's different for women. Geena Davis said that when turned forty it was like 'falling off a cliff'. Her phone suddenly stopped ringing. John Cusack said in an interview that he has actress friends who stopped getting work in their late twenties because by the youth obsessed standards of Hollywood they were already considered old!

By 2003, Lana Clarkson was working as a hostess at the House of Blues in West Hollywood, California. This job was necessary to pay the bills because the acting work was no longer as reliable as it used to be. Lana was living in fairly modest circumstances in a small house and had taken to selling photographs (presumably to B-movie fans) of herself online to make ends meet. At one point she even worked as a children's entertainer to bring in some extra cash. Lana was a good person by all accounts. She did voluntary work for an AIDS charity and always seemed cheerful and kind to people who met her.

On Sunday, February the 2nd, 2003, in what can only be described as a very cruel twist of fate, the shambling music legend Phil Spector arrived at the House of Blues sometime after midnight. Spector ambled into the club wearing one of his ridiculous toupees. Lana Clarkson actually refused him entry at first because she had no idea who he was. Spector had clearly been drinking - which was a bit worrying because he was supposed to be on the wagon. Spector was with another woman that night but she eventually left - leaving him alone. At this point he started chatting to Lana Clarkson - who by now had been informed by other staff members that this diminutive and toupeed character was very famous indeed.

Spector ordered champagne and evidently established a rapport with Clarkson because when her shift ended they left together and went back to his mansion. That would turn out to be the last shift Lana Clarkson ever worked in her life. It was around 2-30 am when they departed from the House of Blues. They are believed to have arrived at Spector's home about 3-30 am. What happened next was something that took two court trials to explain - and even then an element of mystery still remains. It was just a very weird case.
At five-thirty in the morning, after Lana had gone home with

the music icon, Spector emerged from his house carrying a gun and told his limo driver - "I think I just shot her." Spector proved to be tragically accurate with this observation. He had indeed just shot poor Lana Clarkson. Lana was found dead in a chair. She had obviously been shot in the face and head. Her teeth were scattered all around and blood was very evident in the room. Spector was arrested by the police and then released on bail.

There were two trials in the end. The first was judged a mistrial because two members of the jury did not find Spector guilty of murder. They obviously needed a 100% unanimous verdict to convict. The second trial saw the 69 year-old Spector convicted for murder in the second degree. He was sentenced to nineteen years in prison and died in 2021 while still behind bars. Spector cut an eccentric figure in court to say the least. He wore a succession of increasingly bizarre wigs and frequently fired his defence team - not that it made any difference to the eventual outcome.

Spector's defence was that Clarkson had committed 'accidental' suicide by putting the gun in her mouth. Spector argued it was all an accident and not his fault. This claim was clearly not terribly convincing. It transpired in court that Spector had a history of pointing guns at women. It also transpired that his judgement was probably impaired by a head injury he received in the 1970s. Given the fact that the volatile and clearly bonkers Spector was prone to waving guns around and also off the wagon it was probably inevitable that something awful was going to happen in the end. What sort of person takes a woman back to their house and pulls a gun out?

In February 2012, Donna Clarkson, the mother of Lana, settled a civil lawsuit with Spector and his insurance company over the wrongful death of Lana Clarkson. Lana was laid to rest at Beth Olam Cemetery in Los Angeles. Spector lived on for eighteen years after Lana's death. All of this time was spent in prison. When he died he was described by one news outlet as talented but flawed. You could probably describe that morally dubious comment as the understatement of the century.

RONNI CHASEN

Ronni Sue Chasen was born in New York in 1946. She was the sister of the cult horror director and writer Larry Cohen. Chasen was an aspiring actress as a young women but eventually moved behind the scenes and became a Hollywood publicist. Her clients included the likes of Michael Douglas, John Williams, and Natalie Wood. Chasen's specific skill was in orchestrating Oscar campaigns for movies or clients. She was exceptional in these duties and a tireless and cheerful presence in the Los Angeles studio film community.

There are many photographs online of famous faces clutching Oscars with Chasen by their side. It was her hard work behind the scenes promoting movies and stars that made many of these triumphs possible. Chasen was brilliant at her job and loved it too. She loved working in the film industry and never wanted to retire.

On November the 16th, 2010, the 64 year-old Chasen attended the glitzy premiere of the Christina Aguilera and Cher film Burlesque. After midnight, Chasen headed home - which entailed a drive through a wealthy enclave of Beverly Hills. Near the intersection of Whittier Drive and Sunset Boulevard at around 12-30 am, four gunshots were fired through the front passenger seat window of Chasen's Mercedes-Benz car. It is believed the shots were most likely fired as Chasen slowed down in preparation to make a turn.

Two of the bullets struck Chasen in the chest and one hit her in the arm. None of these three bullets were fatal in and of themselves but sadly the same could not be said of a fourth bullet. This bullet struck Chasen in the heart. The bullet to the heart was the killer blow. After the shots, Chasen's car carried on moving for about a third of a mile before it struck a pole and the airbag was deployed. Chasen was obviously in no condition to either steer or stop. She only had minutes to live.

Police officers were quickly on the scene because the sound of gunshots had been reported to them by local residents. Chasen was taken to Cedars-Sinai Medical Center and pronounced dead at 1-12 am. Those who knew Chasen were shocked and upset. She was always such a nice person so it seemed both bizarre and unfair that she had been shot to death. There were two obvious question now. Who had killed Ronni Sue Chasen and why? The early theories concerning Chasen's murder were that this was potentially a violent attempted carjacking or maybe just a random shooting involving some troubled David Berkowitz style lunatic.

Some suggested Chaen's death might have been a consequence of some sort of road rage incident but there was never any evidence to support this. The problem with these theories was that incidents like this were very rare in that specific area. At the time of her murder, Chasen was driving through an area where all the houses were worth many millions. This wasn't a violent crime infested area where people got shot on a daily basis. This was an area with much security and a Batphone type hotline to the police.

The police suspect was a local man named Harold Martin Smith. Smith had some criminal convictions on his slate. He lived in a cheap apartment block in Los Angeles. When the police went to speak to Smith though he pulled out a gun and shot himself. The authorities seemed to conclude that this suicide proved he was guilty of the murder. The police would later say that the gun used in the suicide was the same sort of gun that killed Ronnie Chasen.

Many armchair detectives who have studied this case though contend that Smith probably had nothing to do with Chasen's murder. There was no surveillance or forensic evidence linking him to the crime. The swanky area where Chasen was shot was full of security cameras and yet the police did not pick up any footage of a lone black man (Smith was black) suspiciously driving or lurking around. Others pointed out the rather sad but obvious fact that a black man in this well heeled street at some unearthly hour probably would have attracted the attention of the police.

The police, in what felt like a contradiction to their earlier stance, later seemed to come to similar conclusions and suggest that Chasen's death was just a tragic random incident that will probably never be solved. Some of the frustrated friends and colleagues of Chasen felt that the murder investigation was rather lackadaisical and that the police were too quick to wash their hands of this case.

Because of Chasen's line of work, a number of conspiracy theories concerning her death have inevitably abounded. These include the theory that she was killed by a Russian hitman after a film funded by Russian investment money didn't see a profit. Another theory is that Chasen was killed by a rival movie publicist company because she was too good at her job! There is another theory too that Chasen was murdered after an art deal went wrong. The notion that Chasen was murdered by art dealers sounds as far-fetched as any of the movies she promoted during her career.

Because Chasen was killed with hollow point bullets (which are even more lethal than ordinary bullets) this has only fanned the flames of conspiracies. Some of these claim she was killed by a professional hitman (as opposed to a lone criminal or lunatic). It should be stressed though that the police regarded all of these conspiracy theories to be nonsense. The sadly departed Ronnie Chasen was laid to rest at Hillside Memorial Park and Mortuary in Los Angeles. Among those who attended her funeral were Elliott Gould, Amy Pascal, Joe Roth, Leonard Maltin, Kathleen Kennedy, Robert Forster, and Buzz Aldrin.

CHRISTINE CHUBBUCK

Christine Chubbuck was born in Hudson, Ohio, in 1944. She attended various colleges and gained a degree in broadcasting. She eventually gained work at various television stations and seemed to be doing well. In reality, Christine was not a happy person though. She was self-deprecating about her non-existent love life in public but in private she was very tortured by her inability to find love or even go on a few dates with anyone. She found solace in her family - to whom she was very close. Christine even carried on living at home when she left college.

Christine became a reporter for WXLT (a small ABC affiliate in south-west Florida) and was highly praised for her journalism. Behind the scenes though she was still desperately unhappy and battling depression. It was later speculated that a medical operation Christine had meant she only had a short window where it would be possible for her to give birth to children. Given that her love life was non-existent it seems that Christine was greatly dismayed by the very real prospect that she might now never have a child of her own. It is hard to say if anyone realised the true extent of Christine's unhappiness. Perhaps she was able to hide this by throwing herself into her work.

Chubbock did sterling work in her journalism and tackled important environmental and social issues like conservation and drugs. She was also a volunteer at Sarasota Memorial Hospital. Sadly though, the demons which plagued Christine Chubbuck became too much for her in the end. On July the 15th, 1974, Chubbuck was in the studio reading the local news live on air at around 9-30 in the morning. What happened next was completely unexpected and very shocking.

After a piece about a shooting, Chubbuck said "In keeping with the WXLT practice of presenting the most immediate and complete reports of local blood and guts news, TV 40 presents what is believed to be a television first. In living color, an exclusive coverage of an attempted suicide." She then produced a handgun and shot herself in the head behind her ear before dropping to the floor. It was a live suicide.

The station quickly cut to black as horrified staff members rushed into the studio to check on the fallen Christine. The station then began running a movie for viewers at home. There were obviously astonished viewers at home who had witnessed this tragic live suicide for themselves. They began ringing the station to ask if what they had seen was real or a sick joke. Sadly, it was all too real. Chubbuck had shot herself on live television.

Christine Chubbuck was taken to hospital and pronounced dead several hours later. She was 29 years-old. Christine was later cremated. A film and a documentary have been made about her life. Her family were understandably devastated by her death and it took many years before any of her relatives could bring themselves to make any public comments. It later came to light that before her death Christine had done some research for a proposed piece on suicide and gathered a lot of information on how you might successfully shoot yourself.

One of her fellow workers said Christine had once said to him - 'Wouldn't it be wild if I blew myself away on the air?' The worker in question obviously assumed that Christine was joking. Sadly though, she wasn't. It also transpired that several years previously Christine had tried to take her own life by swallowing pills. Christine Lubbock left a suicide note for her work colleagues in which she described what she had done and expressed her wish that everyone would be able to view the footage of her shooting herself live on air. It was a very weird and sad note.

As for the actual tape of Christine Chubbuck shooting herself live on air, well, there has been a rather ghoulish attempt by some to find the footage but it has never seen the light of day (though copies presumably exist somewhere). It is sometimes wondered if anyone at home taped the incident but this seems like a long shot. Few people had VCRs in those days and why would anyone be taping a local news show at nine-thirty in the morning anyway? Some grainy black and white footage of Christine in the moments before the suicide has allegedly surfaced but - mercifully and thankfully perhaps - the actual act has never been shown or leaked into the public (or 'online' if you prefer) realm.

KURT COBAIN

Kurt Cobain was born in Aberdeen, Washington, in 1967. He said he was a fairly normal child until the age of nine when his parents divorced. After that Kurt Cobain became increasingly moody and unhappy. He suffered greatly from depression in his adult life - which was good for his art but not so good for his mental health. Cobain shot to fame as the lead singer in the punky grunge band Nirvana. Nirvana were sort like a cross between Black Sabbath and The Beatles. If you were a teenager in the early 1990s then there's a very good chance that Nirvana was the primary sonic backdrop to your youth. The band started in the late 1980s but it was in the 1990s when they really became big.

Although he got married to (the singer and actress) Courtney Love and had a daughter, none of this could mitigate Cobain's sense of loneliness and sadness. He overdosed a few times on pills but survived these incidents. Cobain's main problem was his addiction to heroin. Courtney Love used heroin herself but she banned Cobain from using the drug in the house because she felt his addiction was far worse. It was perhaps sadly inevitable that Kurt Cobain, with his history of drug abuse and depression, was not going to make old bones.

Cobain was found dead on the 8th of April 1994 at his home in Seattle. He was 27. Cobain's mother said after his death that she had told him not to join the 'stupid' club. This was a reference to the fact that Janis Joplin and Jimi Hendrix were 27 when they died. At the time of his death, Cobain had just escaped from a drug recovery centre by jumping over the wall. This was a disaster as far as his wellbeing was concerned because Cobain was never going to get better so long as he was addicted to heroin.

Cobain had also purchased a shotgun. He told anyone who asked that he'd purchased the shotgun for protection because burglars had targeted his house. This was a lie. Cobain had purchased the shotgun because he wanted to end his life. Cobain decided that he would not try and overdose on pills this time. He intended to shoot himself and make certain this time. Because he'd fled from the recovery centre his mother and wife were very worried and at one point had no idea where Cobain was. He went home in the end and barricaded himself in the greenhouse above his garage.

For some reason no one bothered to look in the greenhouse when Cobain's house was searched (by this time Cobain's mother had declared him a missing person). That was clearly an oversight. Cobain is believed to have shot himself between the 4th and 5th of April. He propped the shotgun (which looked more like a rifle in terms of its shape) against himself and fired into his head. In one of his suicide notes, Cobain had written 'it's better to burn out than to fade away'. He left his wallet by his side - presumably so that he could be identified after shooting himself in the head.

The police were understandably coy about the circumstances of Cobain's body when he was found. He obviously wasn't in a very pretty state after shooting himself in the head. The police were sensitive to his grieving relatives. Cobain's body was cremated and the ashes were scattered in a number of places around Washington State. To this day fans who weren't even born when Nirvana were in the charts still turn up to Cobain's old house as form of pilgrimage.

Although the sad death of Kurt Cobain seemed a clear case of suicide, a theory that he was murdered has gained a surprising amount of traction in the years since his death. An investigator that was hired to find Cobain when he was missing (just prior to his death) believed that the heroin in his system would have made Cobain incapable of holding a gun sufficiently well to shoot himself. Cobain was still holding the gun when his body was found. Some contend that the force of the gun would have released it from his hands when it was fired.

In 2015 it was reported that Richard Lee, who ran a Seattle public access TV show, was trying to sue the police to release the crime scene photographs of Cobain's death in order to prove that it wasn't suicide. As you might imagine, Kurt's daughter Frances Bean Cobain was pretty appalled by this rather tasteless stunt and along with her mother spoke out to block it. The theory that Kurt Cobain was murdered, if true, does beg an obvious question. Who killed him and why? A troubled fan? It is probably safe to say that, so far at least, the murder theory in relation to Cobain's death is taken with a large dose of salt.

CHRISTIE SCHOEN CODD

Cristie Schoen Codd was born in Madrid in 1976. She was a chef and appeared on the eighth season of the Food Network series Food Network Star. Cristie was involved in the catering on many big budget movies and according to The Hollywood reporter was also a stuntwoman. Blonde and attractive, she was a natural performer on television and seemed destined to become much more famous in the future. In March, 2016, Christie and her husband Joseph were reported missing in Leicester, N.C. by relatives. This was an especially worrying development because Cristie Schoen Codd was pregnant at the time.

When the police went to the couple's home they found some rather odd details which immediately raised their suspicions and didn't make any sense. The couple's cars were still in the drive and the family dogs were also in the house. It was obviously highly unlikely that the couple would just suddenly go away without telling anyone, without transport, and leave their beloved dogs to fend for themselves. This naturally led the police to strongly suspect that foul play might have played a part in this disappearance and - sadly - that assumption turned out to be correct.

The main person of interest in this case was a man named Robert Jason Owens. Owens was a contractor who had recently done some work at the house of Cristie Schoen Codd. The police also learned from a neighbour that there had been some activity at the house which struck them as rather suspicious. They had witnessed a solitary man taking items from the home and putting them in a dumpster. The dumped items that were retrieved by the police were found to belong to Cristie Schoen Codd and her husband. You didn't need to be Sherlock Holmes to deduce that the mysterious man trying to get rid of this stuff was Robert Jason Owens.

The police managed to obtain a warrant to search the home of Robert Jason Owens and made a grim discovery. He had human remains in his woodstove. It turned out that Owens had also stolen a laptop and gun from the Codd home. Owens' wife told the police that her husband had confessed to murdering Joseph Codd. He had clearly killed Christie too. Owens dismembered both of their bodies in an attempt to burn the evidence. He had got pretty far in his grisly operation but the human remains still in the woodstove gave him away.

Owens, who was on heavy medication and suffering from depression, told the police that he had accidentally run over the couple when his truck got stuck in a ditch. He said he tried to burn the bodies because he was frightened that no one would believe it was an accident and he'd be arrested for murder. He said he wanted to make it look like a robbery. It's probably fair to say that this story of Owens did not have much credibility. If you accidentally run someone over you call the emergency services. You don't dismember the bodies and try to burn them.

The details of how the couple really died have never been disclosed. Owens never divulged why he killed the couple. All we can say is that he was a troubled and dangerous man. There was quite likely a financial motivation given that Owens had stolen items from the house. It could be the case that he presumed Christie and her husband might have money in the house somewhere or maybe a safe. There is another theory that Owens was in love with Christie and killed both her and her husband in a jealous rage.

Owens had previously been questioned over the disappearance of a young man in the area though he was never charged with anything because a body nor remains were ever found. In 2000, Zebb Quinn vanished after a night out with Owens. That night Owens visited a hospital for treatment on injuries he said he had obtained in a car crash. However, there was no evidence on his car to suggest an accident. There was a curious incident soon after where Owens called Zebb's place of work pretending to be Zebb and telling them he was sick. It seems pretty obvious that Owens MUST have played a part in Quinn's disappearance.

Owens was sentenced on April the 27th, 2017, to spend a minimum of 59.5 years to a maximum of 74.5 years in prison. His legal team managed to arrange a plea bargain deal (it was hoped that as part of his plea bargain deal that Owens might come clean about what happened to Zebb Quinn but nothing came of this) which avoided the death penalty. Cristie Schoen Codd was 38 at the time of her death. The fact that she was pregnant when murdered added an even greater layer of tragedy into this already sad and tragic case. Christie's devastated family said there was no punishment for Owens that could ever mitigate their sense of loss.

TOMMY COOPER

Tommy Cooper was born in Caerphilly, Glamorgan, Wales, in 1921. Cooper was a beloved British comedian who was a fixture on television for many decades. During the war Cooper served with Montgomery's Eighth Army in Egypt. He started his comedy act while in the services (it was here where Cooper picked up his gimmick of wearing a fez). Cooper's act was that he would play an incompetent magician where all the tricks he tried to do would constantly go wrong. He would also tell amusing corny puns while he did this act. It helped a lot that Cooper looked funny. He was a big shambling man with unruly hair and a huge Desperate Dan chin. He had an unmistakable voice too. Cooper didn't even have to do anything to get laughs. As soon as he shambled onto the stage in his fez and tuxedo people would start laughing. Cooper just had funny bones.

While other comics went in and out of fashion, Cooper just constantly worked. His funny and eccentric bungling magician character was enjoyed by many generations of British television viewers. Behind the scenes, Cooper wasn't in the best of health by the time the 1970s rolled around. He drank and smoked too much and he had all manner of medical issues and ailments. In 1977 he suffered a heart-attack but managed to survive.

It is said that ITV refused to give him another series in 1980 because they were worried about his drinking and felt he had become unreliable. Nonetheless, Cooper still appeared on ITV shows as a guest and was still always in demand himself. On the 15th of April, 1984, the now 63 year-old Tommy Cooper was booked to appear on the ITV variety show Live from Her Majesty's, transmitted live from Her Majesty's Theatre in Westminster, London. As ever, Cooper did his bungling magician act and had the audience roaring with laughter.

The compere of the show that night was the comedian Jimmy Tarbuck. Tarbuck assisted Cooper in a section of the act where Cooper would magically produce items from his gown. The items would get increasingly elaborate so that in the end Cooper would be producing ladders and things of that nature from his gown. The punchline of the trick would be that it was revealed Cooper was being fed these items through the stage curtains behind him by an assistant (who in this instance was Tarbuck). Anyway, this trick always got a big laugh when it was revealed that Cooper was pulling these props from behind the curtain.

It was at this point, about half-way through the trick, that Cooper suddenly slumped to the floor in a heap. Though no one knew it at that precise moment, Cooper had suffered a massive heart-attack and collapsed. He had essentially died on live television right there on the stage. The live studio audience simply assumed it was part of the act though and carried on laughing. Behind the scenes, people were fairly quick to deduce that something had gone wrong and that Cooper's collapse was not part of the act. They pulled him from the stage from behind the curtains and the director of the show instructed the ITV regions to cut to a commercial break. The orchestra suddenly started playing.

Attempts were made to revive Cooper backstage but it was to no avail. The show actually continued while this was happening and a pair of comedians had to go on and do their act while Tommy Cooper was dying only metres away. Paramedics arrived at the theatre but Tommy Cooper could not be saved. He was dead on arrival at Westminster Hospital. There were many warm tributes from the world of comedy when Cooper's death was announced. He had been a great inspiration to many and a towering figure in his field.

Tommy Cooper was cremated at Mortlake Crematorium in London. In 2008, the actor Sir Anthony Hopkins, a big Tommy Cooper fan, unveiled a statue of Cooper in the comedian's birthplace Caerphilly. Tommy Cooper's 'live' death while on stage has often been fairly easy to find on YouTube. This has struck many as rather morbid and distasteful. Tommy Cooper was certainly not the first performer to die on stage and he almost certainly won't be the last.

MARY ANN COTTON

Mary Ann Cotton was born in Sunderland in 1832. She tends to be known as The Black Widow in true crime lore. Cotton has sometimes been called Britain's first serial killer. It's safe to say that if you were ever offered a cup of tea by Mary Ann Cotton you'd be advised to decline unless you enjoy a large dose of arsenic in your PG Tips. Her childhood was fairly uneventful save for her father dying in a mining accident. She spent some time in a boarding school and was said to be a sensible girl who always took a great pride in her appearance. This last quality was evident in her choice of profession. Mary trained to become a dressmaker.

In 1852, Mary married a man named William Mowbray. They had several children but few of them survived. Not all of these births were registered so it was difficult to keep track of exactly how many children they had and how many died. In those days the sad premature death of babies and infants was not uncommon so these deaths were not considered suspicious. Mary's husband William died in 1865 because of a stomach ailment. William was insured and Mary recieved a nice little payment upon his death as a result. Mary's second husband was George Ward. He also died though - once again allowing Mary to collect an insurance payment. The cause of death was cited as cholera but the suddenness of his departure from this vale of tears was rather surprising.

Husband number three for Mary was a widower named James Robinson. Meanwhile, Mary's mother died suddenly after complaining of stomach pains. Yes, you might say that all these sudden deaths in relation to Mary were becoming rather too suspicious. Mary's daughter and two of Robinson's children (from his previous marriage) then all suddenly died in quick succession. James Robinson had noticed at this juncture how Mary kept trying to persuade him to take out life insurance. He decided to boot her out of the house after discovering that she had been pawning his valuables and running up debts.

In 1870, Mary nabbed husband number four when she married Frederick Cotton (from whom she obviously got her last name). Mary was pretty destitute by this point after the collapse of her last marriage and so was desperate to find a new husband. This new marriage was actually illegal because she wasn't even officially divorced from her last husband. Mary wasn't the greatest wife in the world it has to be said. She found out that an old flame named Joseph Nattrass lived nearby and so went off to woo him. As for Frederick Cotton, you can probably guess what happened to him. That's right. He died of a stomach complaint.

Frederick Jr, the child of her last husband, then suddenly died as did Joseph Nattrass - who was Mary's lodger at the time. In 1872, one of Mary Cotton's surviving stepchildren Charles Cotton died suddenly and mysteriously. Mary had told a parish official that Charles 'was in the way' of her future plans. When the apparently healthy Charles dropped dead, the local parish official became highly suspicious (not before time you might argue!) of Mary.

Mary tried to collect the life insurance on Charles but the authorities would not release the money until a medical investigation had taken place. When the body of Charles Cotton was exhumed, arsenic was found in his system. At the trial which followed, Mary was sentenced to death but insisted she was innocent. 'After conviction,' wrote The Times, 'the wretched woman exhibited strong emotion but this gave place in a few hours to her habitual cold, reserved demeanour and while she harbours a strong conviction that the royal clemency will be extended towards her, she staunchly asserts her innocence of the crime that she has been convicted of.'

Mary Ann Cotton was hanged at Durham County Gaol in March 1873. The hanging was rather botched and she ended up slowly choking to death on the rope. Of Mary Ann Cotton's thirteen estimated children, only two survived her. She had killed the vast majority of her family.

DIMEBAG DARRELL

Darrell Lance Abbott was born in Ennis, Texas, in 1966. He was better known as Dimebag Darrell. He was the guitarist of the heavy metal bands Pantera and Damageplan. Darrell was regarded to be one of the great heavy metal guitarists. On December the 8th, 2004, the 38 year-old Darrell was on stage with his band Damageplan at the Alrosa Villa nightclub in Columbus, Ohio. The band were still only on their first song of the set when a 26 year-old man named Nathan Gale clambered onto the stage. People jumping onto the stage during a heavy metal show is nothing new or unusual but it was a bit odd to see someone doing it during the first song. It quickly became apparent though why Gale had wasted no time in invading the stage. He was a man on a most harrowing mission.

Gale, who emerged from the amps at the side of the stage, had a handgun and - to the horror of all who could see what was happening - he shot Dimebag Darrell several times. Darrell was hit by four bullets in all. One of the bullets had no exit point and lodged in his head. The band's chief bodyguard rushed to the stage to grapple Gale but was fatally shot in the process. A fan who tried to intervene and protect the band was also shot. Erin Halk, who worked in the arena was also shot and killed. The band's tour manager also took a bullet in the chaos. It had turned into a mass shooting. Nathan Gale was a spree killer. He was perfectly willing to shoot anyone who came into his sight.

Three people in the crowd were also wounded before a police officer entered the arena and shot Gale dead. This was a merciful intervention because heaven knows how many people Gale might have killed if he'd been left to his own devices for any longer. It was obviously very difficult for anyone to apprehend him because to even attempt to do this ran the risk of being shot. Gale seemed to know what he was doing to when it came to using the gun. This was no amateur. The reason why he was competent with a handgun would become apparent in the aftermath of the case when more was known about him.

The police officer who killed Gale was James Niggemeyer. Niggemeyer took only three minutes to respond to the first emergency call and shot Gale in the head with a Remington shotgun. Given that Gale had gone crazy and was shooting anyone who went near him this police officer almost certainly saved lives that night. Niggemeyer suffered from severe post-traumatic stress disorder after the incident and quit the police force in the end. He fired from fairly long range because he was confident he could make the shot. He probably didn't have much choice because if he'd delayed for longer someone else probably would have been killed. There was an investigation into Niggemeyer's use of deadly force but he was cleared of any blame or use of excessive force.

Dimebag Darrell had been shot at point blank range in the head, face, and ear. He had no chance of surviving these bullets at such close range and was shortly pronounced dead. What made this death even more tragic is that Damageplan were almost at the end of the tour. This was their second to last show. Nathan Gale had some previous with the band in that he'd invaded the stage before during one of their shows and destroyed some equipment. The band elected not to press charges at the time and quickly forgot about the incident. Sadly, Gale would be back at their concerts again - this time with deadly and tragic consequences.

It has been alleged that Gale was furious at Dimebag Darrell because he judged the guitarist to be responsible for breaking up Pantera. Some allege that Gale shouted as much on stage before he shot the guitarist. This has never been verified though. Other members of Damageplan on stage that fateful night say that they could see that Gale was shouting something before the shooting but it was too loud in the arena to actually hear him or decipher what he was actually ranting about.

It turned out that Nathan Gale had served in the United States Marine Corps. This is why he was so deadly with a gun. Gale was discharged from the Marines for reasons that were never explained. It is believed he suffered from paranoid schizophrenia and had some issues with substance abuse. He was clearly a troubled man who had finally tilted over the edge into madness. Gale previously played semi-pro football for the Lima Thunder. It is said that he listened to Pantera before each match.

The murder of Darrell Lance Abbott led to many music venues and bands revamping their security measures. For a long time many people in bands were very wary of anyone who tried to get up on the stage. You certainly can't blame them for this. Any musician who goes up on the stage should feel safe. Darrell was laid to rest at the Moore Memorial Gardens Cemetery, Arlington, Tarrant County, Texas. There were many warm tributes from the world of music to this talented guitarist.

The family of Dimebag Darrell investigated a lawsuit against the club where he died for not offering sufficient protection. The owner of the club argued, not unreasonably, that his staff were not trained nor expected to battle gun wielding maniacs who jump on the stage trying to shoot the band. This was just a very shocking and bizarre incident that thankfully is the exception rather than the rule.

JAMES DEAN

James Dean was born in Marion, Indiana, in 1931. Although he only made a handful of films, Dean became an enduring icon of the screen. He was one of the first people to introduce the concept of youthful rebellion to popular culture and film and his early death at the age of 24 only enhanced his status as a slightly unfathomable but effortlessly cool cult star. Though they operated in different fields of entertainment, Dean is felt to have been a huge influence on stars like Elvis. James Dean had a timeless sort of quality which (if this isn't a contradiction) made him feel ahead of his time.

Of the three films Dean starred in (he had earlier uncredited roles in a number of movies and also appeared in some television productions) he only lived long enough to actually see one of them released. Dean was artistic as a child but when he got a bit older the thing he loved most of all was to ride his motorcycle. His love of speed would - quite literally - be the death of him. Dean enrolled in college but dropped out early. He headed for New York to study acting and after this began to pick up some work in commercials. He also appeared on the stage during his promising but sadly truncated acting career.

Dean purchased a Porsche Spyder and began to participate in road races. His acting career received a huge boost when he was cast in East of Eden - an adaptation of John Steinbeck's 1952 novel. The producers had wanted Brando for the role of Caleb but took a punt on the unknown Dean instead. Dean's sensitive and often improvised performance won him a posthumous Oscar. Dean took on an even more famous role next as Jim Stark in Rebel Without a Cause. This film was an early and original example of teen angst. It also featured two other doomed icons in Natalie Wood and Sal Mineo.

Dean's next film was Giant - which was released posthumously. Dean also earned another Oscar nomination for this film although (once again) he obviously wasn't around to enjoy that. Dean played a Texas rancher in the movie. It was notable that this was a different sort of part for him. He was already conscious of being typecast and so wanted to move away from moody teen roles. Dean was given a big studio contract now which promised to make him very wealthy. There were plans for Dean to play the boxer Rocky Graziano in the biopic Somebody Up There Likes Me. Alas though, this plan, like all of James Dean's plans, never came to pass. Graziano was instead played by a young actor named Paul Newman.

On September the 30th, 1955, Dean headed for Salinas in his Porsche. He was due there to take part in a race. The car was originally going to be transported by trailer but Dean changed his mind about this and decided to drive it there himself. This is what you might call a twist of fate. The decision to drive the car there himself would come at the cost of James Dean's life. One of the darkly ironic things about Dean is that one of the last things he ever did was appear in a public information film about road safety where he warned teenagers to drive sensibly.

Also in the car on that fateful day was Dean's mechanic Rolf Wütherich. On U.S. Route 466 near Cholame, California, at approximately 5:45 p.m, Dean had a collision with a Ford car driven by a student named Donald Turnupseed. The Ford made a turn which gave Dean no time to stop or evade the vehicle. Dean's car slammed into the side of the Ford. Wütherich (who survived despite broken bones) was thrown out of the car by the impact and Donald Turnupseed, though shocked and shaken, was not badly hurt and able to walk from his car. The same could not be said for James Dean. He was trapped in the car and suffered bad injuries - including a broken neck.

Dean's Porsche was thrown into the air and landed on its side. It was a terribly violent crash. The car was thrown clean off the road and came to a stop by a telegraph pole. Photographs of the car after the crash show it smashed in like a folded accordion and the roof ripped off. Dean had been terribly mangled in the crash. His arms were broken and he had internal injuries. Earlier that day Dean had received a ticket for speeding. It is somewhat ironic that he was driving fairly slowly and sensibly when this tragic crash occurred. It was erroneously reported that Dean was doing an average of 90 mph at the time of the crash but a police report stated that he driving on average closer to 50 mph.

James Dean was ferried by ambulance to Paso Robles War memorial Hospital but his injuries were so catastrophic there was no hope of saving him and he was pronounced dead on arrival. His funeral service took place at Fairmount Friends Church and he was buried in Fairmount's Park Cemetery. Elizabeth Taylor, who had become friends with Dean working on the film Giant, sent flowers. Though his fame was growing at the time of his passing it was only really in death that Dean became a full fledged icon. He is now forever frozen in time as that moody, bequiffed and charismatic young man. As for Rolf Weutherich, he died in a car crash in 1981. He was evidently not so lucky this time around.

There are conspiracy theories that Dean faked his death through the crash to go and live a quiet life without fame but these are not taken very seriously. One spooky true story though is that, about a week before his death, Dean had lunch with the actor Alec Guinness. Dean showed Alec Guiness his Porsche and Guiness had a dreadful premonition that Dean would be killed in that car. He told James Dean not to drive the car. Dean obviously this ignored this advice though. If he'd listened to Alec Guinness the crash never would have happened.

KRISTIAN DIGBY

Kristian Digby was born in Devon in 1977. Digby became best known for hosting the BBC property show To Buy or Not to Buy. He also worked as a presenter on Living In The Sun, House Swap and Buy It, Sell It, Bank It. Digby was a familiar face on British television and fairly well known. If you watched television in Britain during the time that Digby was active then you almost certainly would have encountered him somewhere or other. He was all over the place.

Digby supported both dyslexia charities and LGBT charities and had also made some documentaries. Of his sexuality, Digby said - "I don't have to do innuendo and keep referring to my sexuality all the time and making it blatantly obvious that I am gay, because it's not that important. I love gay culture but we need to show that we're more diverse. We keep limiting ourselves." Digby was also famous for his property interests - famously building a stylish minimalist home in the garden of one of his existing properties in East London. This home was where Digby lived.

On the 28th of Febuary, 2010, Digby's partner Jason Englebrecht arrived back in England after a trip to South Africa but found it odd that he couldn't seem to contact Digby on the phone or by message. He therefore used his phone to ask a neighbour of Digby to check on Kristian. The neighbour found Kristian Digby dead in his bed. It was the 1st of March, 2010. Digby was just 32 years-old. He was found with a plastic bin liner over his head which was held in place by a belt. Next to him was an ethyl chloride spray. Ethyl chloride is a local anaesthetic. Acute brief inhalation of this substance can result in feeling of drunkenness, euphoria, and hallucinations.

The coroner recorded a verdict of death by misadventure. This was clearly a case of autoerotic asphyxiation. Autoerotic asphyxiation is among the strangest and most dangerous sexual kinks. It basically involves starving oneself of oxygen to heighten sexual arousal. This act is incredibly risky because if if it goes wrong you will die. There was no suspicion of foul play or third party involvement in the death. Digby had died alone.

A number of celebrities have died in this strange way and Kiristian Digby was merely the latest. For understandable reasons, relatives of the deceased and the police and medical authorities tend to - in official terms - skirt around autoerotic asphyxiation deaths and offer a more generic and vague explanation in public. It is just a very embarrassing sort of way to die and the mourning relatives don't really want it broadcast to all and sundry in the media.

Britain had already experienced a high profile death by autoerotic asphyxiation in 1994 when Stephen Milligan, a Member of Parliament (MP) in the Conservative Party, was found dead in his house in London. The 45 year-old Milligan was wearing women's underwear, had an electrical flex around his neck, and an orange in his mouth. There was initially speculation that Milligan had been bound and gagged and murdered by someone but this wasn't the case at all. It was simply an attempt at autoerotic asphyxiation which had gone badly and tragically wrong. Most people presumed that Milligan had hung himself and was unhappy. None of this was true.

Those who had worked with Kristian or knew him were shocked by his sudden and strange death. Dominic Littlewood, who was Kristian Digby's co-presenter on To Buy or Not to Buy, said - "There's not a bad word I can say about Kristian. He was a lovely, fun, nice, jolly, decent person." Julian Bennett, who also worked with Digby, said - "He did so much for the gay community. He appealed to the masses. He was well educated. He made gay acceptable to the middle class and that was a tough thing to do. Being gay has never been a problem for him. He was a gentleman." It seems inevitable that Digby, who was handsome and ambitious, would have become a primetime television star had lived. Sadly, this would never come to pass now.

DIANA DORS

In her youth Diana Dors was sort of regarded to be Britain's version of Marilyn Monroe and under contract to film studios in both Britain and the United States. She was symbolic of a post-war yearning for glamour and flaunted her money and blonde bombshell looks and figure. The young Diana Dors would have been a tabloid fixture to rival anyone today with her marriages, affairs (everyone from Rod Steiger to Bob Monkhouse), her powder-blue Cadillac, wild parties, and the criminal connections of some of the men who passed through her colourful life.

Dors was born Diana Fluck (you can see why she had to change her name) in Swindon in 1931. She studied at the London Academy of Music and Dramatic Art and appeared in films for Rank, later coming under contract to RKO and moving to Hollywood. Despite the Monroe tag the closer parallel is probably Jayne Mansfield who, like Dors, sort of created a character to play. Make no mistake, Diana Dors could act too. She wasn't just a pretty face.

Yield to the Night, a poignant and sadly forgotten 1956 black and white British film directed by J Lee Thompson, is a case in point. The film was inspired by the story of Ruth Ellis (the last woman to be hanged in Britain) and is a powerful and haunting rejection of capital punishment in a civilised society. It features a remarkable performance by a young Diana Dors, cast against type as the doomed Mary Hilton, sentenced to hang for shooting a woman who she believes drove her lover Jim Lancaster (Michael Craig) to suicide by having an affair with him behind her back and then leaving him.

Yield to the Night begins in striking fashion with Mary shooting her lover's other woman dead in public and then defiantly waiting for the police to arrive. Dors makes a classic fifties femme fatal here but when the story switches to the prison a transformation takes place. Dors, without make-up and in drab prison garb, suddenly appears younger, prettier and a lot more vulnerable. It's a surprisingly moving and natural performance and, although it seems this film has been somewhat forgotten, Yield to the Night must surely stand as Diana Dors finest hour. Dors is great in the prison scenes: resigned, sulky, bored, scared, depressed, hopeful, delirious, philosophical and always very human.

When Diana Dors lived in Hollywood, numerous famous names (Doris Day, Debbie Reynolds etc) were guests at swanky parties at her house but Dors soon began to stretch the patience of RKO. Her first husband Denis Hamilton beat her 'black and blue' according to a biographer and would turn down film roles on her behalf without telling her. He wrecked her Hollywood career by kicking a photographer in the head during an infamous pool party incident. Offers to work with Robert Mitchum and Jerry Lewis vanished and she was effectively blackballed in Hollywood, considered too much trouble and prone to affairs and wayward behaviour.

It's actually quite difficult at times to keep up with the full tumult of Dors' life - which took in three marriages, dozens of affairs and lovers, abortion, custody battles over children, debt, bankruptcy, media gossip and battles with illness until her premature death at the age of 52. Dors' early notoriety stemmed from stories fed to the press by Hamilton. Her exploits and dress sense would seem rather tame today but it was cheeky stuff back then. In 1960 she was criticised by the archbishop of Canterbury Dr Geoffrey Fisher for being a bad role model after some of her memoirs were published in a newspaper.

At the height of her fame, Dors was turning down Bob Hope films because she didn't want to dye her hair, having an affair with Rod Steiger, appearing on American chat shows and living in a villa off Sunset Boulevard. She even brought out a couple of records and appeared on the Beatles' Sgt Pepper's Lonely Hearts Club Band album cover. Her looks though were inevitably not going to last forever The film roles were drying up and Dors had started to put weight on. Britain's answer to Marilyn Monroe would end up being cast as the nagging dowdy wife in low-budget seventies comedy and horror films.

The Inland Revenue went after Dors for £40,000 in the sixties. Her reaction to a tax bill that she knew would wipe her out was to throw a fireworks party and practically burn her house down in the process! Dors was notorious for hosting 'sex parties' and drugs were rife in her home. Despite this she retained a warm image and was something of a British institution in her last years and a fixture on breakfast television. It was therefore something of a shock when she passed away in 1984 after a recurrence of ovarian cancer. Diana Dors might have left the party a trifle early but you can't say that she didn't make the most of her time.

R.BUDD DWYER

R. Budd Dwyer was born in St. Charles, Missouri, in 1929. He served from 1965 to 1971 as a Republican member of the

Pennsylvania House of Representatives and from 1971 to 1981 as a member of the Pennsylvania State Senate representing the state's 50th district. Dwyer then served as the 30th treasurer of Pennsylvania. Though not terribly well known outside of Pennsylvania, Dwyer's profile was boosted in the most tragic circumstances possible. It was the bizarre and gruesome manner of his death which briefly made him famous.

The source of Dwyer's trouble all came from that fact that some state taxes had been overpaid in a previous administration. Those who had paid too much were now entitled to some compensation. To cut a long story short, Dwyer was then accused of accepting a bribe from the company who were awarded the contract to handle all the compensation claims. He was found guilty of conspiracy, mail fraud, perjury, and interstate transportation in aid of racketeering. Dwyer was facing not only political ruin but a lengthy spell in prison (the American legal system is famously harsh on financial crimes). Prosecutors said that Dwyer had taken a $300,000 bribe from the company who were awarded the overpaid taxes contract. Dwyer, to put it mildly, was devastated by this turn of events and furious at his treatment.

Dwyer insisted to anyone who would listen that he was innocent and insisted this was a grave miscarriage of justice. He turned down a plea bargain deal in which he would have pleaded guilty and then only been charged with one minor offence. It was probably not a terribly logical decision to reject this deal because he now faced the possibility of 55 years in prison. He should have taken the plea bargain. Dwyer was in no mood to admit to anything though. He was determined to see this through to the bitter end. Dwyer was especially angry that the (somewhat more pragmatic) company bosses who were awarded the compensation contract testified against him in return for lesser charges. Dwyer felt like he had been stabbed in the back.

On January the 22nd, 1987, Dwyer arranged a press conference to discuss his case. His advisors were not too happy about this because he was still due to be sentenced and they didn't think that Dwyer blowing off steam at a public event would do him much good. Though they had no way of knowing it, Dwyer planned to do far worse than rail against the American justice system. Journalists and those involved in the legal system simply presumed that Dwyer had called the press conference to announce his resignation as State Treasurer. Dwyer had no intention of doing this though. He was about to do something unfathomably horrific instead.

Dwyer began by reading out a prepared statement in which he continued to claim he was innocent of all charges. He aimed a few barbs at the judge who had sentenced him and implored the media to vindicate him and help prove his innocence. Dwyer's words were sort of predictable up to this point. He was saying what people had expected him to say. Dwyer stopped speaking in the end and handed some of his officials sealed envelopes. Earlier he had told reporters who were going to leave to stay and keep their cameras rolling. Dwyer then produced a Magnum handgun from an envelope.

The mood in the room was now one of horror and anxiety. His staff pleaded with him to put the gun down or give it to them. "Please, please leave the room if this will ... if this will affect you," said Dwyer and then put the gun in his mouth and shot himself. It all happened very quickly. As you can probably imagine, it was a gruesome and distressing thing to witness. There was blood all over the place. Dwyer was killed instantly. He slumped to the floor in a heap with blood gushing from his mouth and nose.

It seems to be something of an urban myth that Dwyer shot himself on live television. Although there were TV cameras there which recorded his harrowing suicide the press conference wasn't being run live by anyone in particular. The weird thing is that one station actually later showed the suicide and even defended its decision to do so. You can't imagine that anyone would do that today. The footage and images shown by the media concerning Dwyer's suicide sparked a debate over what is appropriate or decent to broadcast in news coverage. You can, should morbid curiosity get the better of you, find footage or gifs of Dwyer's suicide online.

As for R. Budd Dwyer, he was buried at Blooming Valley Cemetery. His staff later said that he had seemed like a broken man in his final days. They could obviously have had no way of knowing that he planned to shoot himself at a press conference though. The last part of Dwyer's speech had been rambling and strange. He compared himself to a figure from the Bible. R. Budd Dwyer was simply a man at the end of his tether. This manifested itself in the most horrific way imaginable. It is believed that that a salient reason why he shot himself on his last day of work is that it meant his family would then be entitled to government benefits.

After his death, Dwyer's family continued to argue that he was innocent and even helped produce a documentary to this end. What had made Dwyer suspicious in the first place is that he had awarded the compensation claim contract to a little known and inexperienced company who had actually tendered the least cost effective bid. This decision didn't make much sense and obviously came across as a bit fishy to the authorities. Added to that was the fact that Dwyer had changed the rules so that he was the ONLY person who could decide who got the contract. There is also the fact that Dwyer did try to negotiate a plea bargain where he would confess but prosecutors didn't agree to this because Dwyer wanted all charges dropped in return for divulging information about the bribe. The evidence against him was very strong but, as we have just noted, his surviving relatives still insist he was innocent.

CHRIS FARLEY

Chris Farley was born in Chicago, Illinois, in 1964. He was a comic performer and actor best known for appearing on

Saturday Night Live from 1990 to 1996. Farley then made the switch to movies and appeared in films like Tommy Boy, Black Sheep, and Beverley Hills Ninja. At the time of his death he was preparing to be the main voice actor in Shrek. Farley had to be replaced by Mike Myers when he passed away.

Farley's hero was John Belushi. It was Belushi who had inspired Farley to get into comedy and become a performer. Sadly though he emulated Belushi all too well - both of these comic performers dying far too young thanks to drugs. Belushi became a star through Saturday Night Live and then moved into films with National Lampoon's Animal House and then The Blues Brothers with his friend Dan Akroyd. He had huge problems with drugs though and died in 1982 after a huge binge that ended with a 'speedball' of cocaine and heroin. At the time of Belushi's death, Akroyd had been writing Ghostbusters as a vehicle for himself and Belushi - the late Belushi eventually replaced by Bill Murray in the film.

Farley died on December the 17th, 1997. He was famously overweight so not the healthiest person in the world to start with. Added to this were his battles with drink and drugs. It was probably inevitable that without drastic changes to his lifestyle Chris Farley was never going to make old bones. At the time of his death, Farley was in Chicago. He had purchased an apartment in the John Hancock Building. This is an iconic tower in Chicago which was used in the movie Poltergeist III. Farley lived on the 60th floor. Farley had hooked up with a prostitute named Heidi and was in the midst of an epic and ultimately fatal and destructive drugs bender. He hadn't slept for days.

Farley had gone to Heidi's apartment at one point but then they ended up back in his place. He used crack and heroin during this prolonged and deadly binge. In the end Heidi became frustrated that Farley hadn't given her any money and left. Farley was lying on the floor in a sorry state when she departed. You'd probably have grounds to suggest that Heidi shouldn't have left Farley alone in such a terrible mess but she'd clearly had enough by this point. Maybe she just assumed he would sleep it off and wake up none the worse for wear. She probably wasn't thinking that straight herself after all the drink and drugs.

Farley's brother found Chris the next morning. He was wearing only pyjama bottoms and was inert. There was foam and liquid coming from his mouth. An ambulance was called but it was too late. Chris Farley was pronounced dead. He was 33 years-old - the exact age that John Belushi had been when he died from a drugs binge. Farley's cause of death was cited as morphine and cocaine intoxication. There were opened bottles of booze and prescription drugs all around the apartment. One obviously presumes that the authorities also found illegal narcotics.

It is doubtful that anyone could have survived the drugs bender that Chris Farley had undertaken. Farley's last completed movie was Almost Heroes. Sadly this film turned out to be a dud and was a rare case of Christopher Guest making a bad picture. It was released posthumously. Chris Farley had been to rehab many times but sadly was never able to stick at it long enough to get clean and sober. His poor health had become increasingly apparent in some of his last public appearances on television. He was bigger than ever and seemed hoarse and tired. There was a sweaty desperation to Farley's last performances. It was clear that he was struggling to summon forth his usual manic energy.

Farley's funeral was a star studded event full of famous faces from the world of comedy. Farley's friend and comedy partner David Spade was notably absent though - which led to speculation the pair had fallen out before Farley died. Spade later said though that he didn't go because he simply couldn't face it. He was too distraught. Chris Farley's remains were interred at Resurrection Cemetery in Madison. At the time of his death he had many film projects in the pipeline. If he had managed to conquer his demons and get healthy he could have been a much bigger star. Farley will always be remembered though for his stint on Saturday Night Live.

ALBERT FISH

Albert Fish was born in Washington, D.C. in 1870. If every age has its own bogeyman then it can be said that Albert Fish took on this role in the early decades of the 20th century. He molested over 400 children and tortured and killed others. We will never know exactly how many people Fish might have killed. Albert Fish said his greatest pleasure in life was to inflict pain. Fish grew-up in an orphanage and the regular beatings the children received there seemed to activate a sadomasochistic enjoyment of pain (both giving and receiving) in Fish. Fish liked to be hit with a spiked cane as an adult. As a boy he was a Peeping Tom and when he began experimenting with homosexual relationships he discovered that he enjoyed watersports. And no, I don't mean water skiing.

One of the strangest things about the disturbing life of Albert Fish is that he got married and had six children. This marriage was arranged by his mother but Fish was said to be a good father - despite the fact that in his private life he was out raping boys. He landed in prison a few times for theft but his more serious crimes seemed to evade the notice of the authorities - for a time at least. Fish moved from New York to Wilmington around this time. His occupation was a house painter and this often meant he had to travel to get some work. In Wilmington he began a secret relationship with a teenager named Thomas Keddon. Fish cut off the genitals of Keddon and left him bleeding and tied up in a farmhouse. No one is sure what happened to Keddon in the end.

Fish claimed that he killed and raped other children in the period that followed. There was an incident where he stabbed a mentally handicapped boy and he killed a child named Francis McDonnell. The flesh from one of the child's legs had been hacked away. Fish always claimed to be a cannibal. He once told the police that he made a stew out of the nose and ears of one of his victims. No wonder Albert Fish is considered to have been one of the inspirations for Hannibal Lecter.

The most infamous crime of Fish came when he pretended to be hiring farm workers and met the Budd family (whose father Edward was seeking employment). Fish persuaded them to let their ten year-old daughter Grace visit him to attend a birthday party for his niece but - of course - it was all a ruse and Grace turned up to find Fish alone. Fish later sent the Budd family a letter in which he claimed to have cooked and eaten Grace after he killed her.

'My dear Mrs Budd, In 1894 a friend of mine shipped as a deck hand on the steamer Tacoma, Capt John Davis. They sailed from San Francisco to Hong Kong China. On arriving there he and two others went ashore and got drunk. When they returned the boat was gone. At that time there was a famine in China. Meat of any kind was from $1 to 3 Dollars a pound. So great was the suffering among the very poor that all children under 12 were sold to the Butchers to be cut up and sold for food in order to keep others from starving. A boy or girl under 14 was not safe in the street. You could go in any shop and ask for steak – chops – or stew meat. Part of the naked body of a boy or girl would be brought out and just what you wanted cut from it. A boy or girls behind which is the sweetest part of the body and sold as veal cutlet brought the highest price. John staid there so long he acquired a taste for human flesh. On his return to N.Y. he stole two boys one 7 one 11. Took them to his home stripped them naked tied them in a closet then burned everything they had on. Several times every day and night he spanked them – tortured them – to make their meat good and tender. First he killed the 11 yr old boy, because he had the fattest ass and of course the most meat on it. Every part of his body was cooked and eaten except Head – bones and guts. He was roasted in the oven, (all of his ass) boiled, broiled, fried, stewed.

'The little boy was next, went the same way. At that time I was living at 409 E 100 St, rear – right side. He told me so often how good human flesh was I made up my mind to taste it. On Sunday June the 3 – 1928 I called on you at 406 W 15 St. Brought you pot cheese – strawberries. We had lunch. Grace sat in my lap and kissed me. I made up my mind to eat her, on the pretence of taking her to a party. You said Yes she could go. I took her to an empty house in Westchester I had already picked out. When we got there, I told her to remain outside. She picked wild flowers. I went upstairs and stripped all my clothes off. I knew if I did not I would get her blood on them. When all was ready I went to the window and called her. Then I hid in a closet until she was in the room. When she saw me all naked she began to cry and tried to run down stairs. I grabbed her and she said she would tell her mama. First I stripped her naked. How she did kick – bite and scratch. I choked her to death then cut her in small pieces so I could take my meat to my rooms, cook and eat it. How sweet and tender her little ass was roasted in the oven. It took me 9 days to eat her entire body. I did not **** her, though, I could of [sic] had I wished. She died a virgin.'

The awful mocking letter that Albert Fish wrote to the Budd family sealed his fate. The authorities were able to deduce that Fish used stationary from the New York Private Chauffeur's Benevolent Association (Fish was actually working as a chauffeur at the time) and managed to find out where he was living. Fish died in the electric chair in 1936. He seemed to welcome the chance to sample the electric chair. Fish said it would be a great thrill. X-rays taken of Fish when he was in custody revealed twenty needles he had pushed into his groin. He was a seriously strange and disturbing man. Albert Fish is sometimes called The Werewolf of Wysteria in true crime articles now. The autograph of Fish sold for $30,000 in 2010 on a true crime website.

F.SCOTT FITZGERALD

F. Scott Fitzgerald was born in Saint Paul, Minnesota, in 1896. Fitzgerald was 23 when This Side of Paradise was published and it launched him into an early stardom that would burn bright before fading out to a relatively early grave. This was all hastened by booze. Fitzgerald could stay sober and clear headed for periods when he was writing but once he'd had a few gins there was frequently no stopping him. When his famous "flapper" wife Zelda ended up in a sanatorium it wasn't a great aid to Fitzgerald's sobriety. The money it cost and his daughter's private education meant that near the end of his short life one of America's greatest writers was reduced to writing for the film industry in Hollywood purely to vanquish his debts. "Write well, Mr Fitzgerald! Write well!" said Joan Crawford at a party when she heard he was working on a screenplay for a film of hers. He probably felt like strangling her.

Although he went to Princeton and a nice school, Fitzgerald seemed to have a strange sense of himself even in the champagne drenched circles he loved and moved amongst as something of a figurehead. He considered himself to be less socially privileged (in terms of his background) than many of his peers and so regarded himself an outsider even in the midst of a well-heeled movement that had him at the forefront. This of course played a big part in his fiction with his characters and books obsessed with wealth and background. Old money and new money. There was a big difference between the two.

The Beautiful and Damned was published in 1922 and further established Fitzgerald as a shooting star in the world of fiction. The story concerns a socialite named Anthony Patch who is waiting for his grandfather to die so that he can claim his inheritance. The book chronicles his relationship with his wife Gloria (regarded to be a thinly veiled Zelda by many readers) and his battle with drink. One can see why the book is felt to be autobiographical. Fitzgerald was apt to ransacking his own life for material and even used Zelda's diaries sometimes to convey the stormy and complicated nature of maintaining a marriage in fiction.

The Great Gatsby, Fitzgerald's masterpiece, was published in 1925. It's a short novel but generally regarded to be one of the greatest works of fiction of the last century. The story is set during the early part of the Roaring Twenties, the Jazz Age. A time of great prosperity for America. Wild parties, prohibition, bootleggers, new money, people becoming rich. It isn't destined to last though. The great stock market crash of 1929 is just around the corner and will serve as the sober hangover and symbolic ending for this glitter strewn decade of excess. The shadows are already beginning to loom well before in the story. It's an era that can't possibly last forever. So the novel is a snapshot of the age amongst a particular money washed strata of American society before it all goes belly up. These people are distracted by ephemera and can never seem to see the big picture.

Tender is the Night was published in 1933 and is Fitzgerald's last completed novel. There are two different versions of the novel. The original version has a flashback structure but the revised edition - compiled from notes left by Fitzgerald - eschews this device and is more chronological. Although it doesn't make a huge difference to the merit of the book one way or another, it is obvious that the revised edition is Fitzgerald's preferred version and was probably a reaction to the some sniffy reviews of the structural composition he used in the first incarnation of the book.

The story concerns a psychoanalyst named Dick Diver and his complex relationship with his wealthy wife Nicole (yet another Zelda proxy). Nicole is haunted by a dark family secret while Dick comes under the suspicious gaze of Nicole's sister - who wonders if Dick's marriage to her sister is more about money than love. Nicole's money has been very useful to Dick in setting himself up in business with fancy clinics and all. The pair take a house in the South of France where they flit around with other wealthy Americans and enjoy the life of wealthy professional people at play. Strains in their marriage are threatened though when Dick begins a tentative romance with an actress named Rosemary Hoyt. This triggers further drama and much reflection and soul-searching.

The Love of The Last Tycoon is an unfinished novel compiled and published (posthumously) in 1941. It was edited by Fitzgerald's friend (the literary critic) Edmund Wilson and published in 1941 as The Last Tycoon. The Love of The Last Tycoon is said to have been Fitzgerald's preferred title for the novel and it was later thrown out in the world again with that longer title. Fitzgerald was about half-way through the story and apparently was happy with the way it was going but it's a difficult book to assess and judge fairly for understandable and obvious reasons. Would this have been the novel that restored Fitzgerald to his former glory? On the evidence of these fragments the answer is that while The Last Tycoon would have been an impressive novel but it's difficult to say whether it would have been the absolute masterpiece that the author might have been hoping for to signal that he was back as a literary force.

By this stage of his career Fitzgerald was sort of like the forgotten champ, back in training trying to come out of retirement for another shot at the title. Because he had written The Great Gatsby at such a young age there was probably nowhere to go but down. The Last Tycoon is interesting because of its different perspectives and the way the author is trying to experiment and not allow himself to be tied down to any predictable style. It's also fascinating to see Fitzgerald try something new and try to write a great novel about the Hollywood studio system rather than socialites lazing around grand houses or foreign shores.

Despite his current status as the old champ of days gone by, Fitzgerald of course would have been mortified if anyone had ever regarded him to be a hack or someone who's best work was behind him. The hack part of the equation was probably never going to happen but it was a sad fact that his golden years seemed a long time ago now and he was regarded to be somewhat drink addled and financially troubled - hence his stint in Hollywood trying to clear his debts. Fitzgerald died of occlusive coronary arteriosclerosis at 44 years of age in 1940. He was said to be eating a chocolate bar when he suddenly collapsed. Sadly, he could not be revived. He was buried at the Old Saint Mary's Catholic Church Cemetery Rockville, Montgomery County, Maryland.

CAROLINE FLACK

Caroline Flack was born in Enfield in 1979. She was a prolific British television presenter best known for hosting The X Factor and Love Island. This was only the tip of the iceberg though when it came to her broadcasting career. Flack had hosted all manner of stuff down the years. She also won the twelfth series of the BBC's Strictly Come Dancing. Flack was one of the most familiar faces on British television at the time of her death. She seemed to have everything. She was wealthy, in demand, and hugely famous. It felt like her broadcasting career still had decades to run. Her past boyfriends included Prince Harry, Harry Styles, and the rugby player Danny Cipriani. She was seen as a glamourous sort of figure in the world of television.

However, in private she wasn't the most stable or happy person and suffered from severe mental health problems. It is said that one thing Caroline Flack could never quite cope with is the abuse that many celebrities have to endure online and on social media on a daily basis. As she was a television presenter famed for hosting shows which, while wildly popular with millions of viewers, were considered (with respect) rather trashy and low-brow, Flack was obviously someone who got her fair share of criticism both from professional critics and also troll idiots on social media. If you are in the public eye these days in the manner that Flack was you just have to ignore all this stuff or develop a thick skin. Caroline was evidently not able to do either of these things.

The source of Flack's final descent into fatal depression was a big bust up with her boyfriend Lewis Burton in 2019. Flack attacked him while he was asleep because she suspected he had been cheating on her. When the police arrived to investigate they found Flack covered in blood. It obviously wasn't her blood either. It was Burton's blood. Flack, much to her dismay, had to make court appearances in relation to this incident and the newspapers were naturally all over this story like fleas on a cat. She suffered great stress during this period and had to stand down as the host of Love Island. The assumption was that Flack would return to the show once this personal strife was over but that would never happen.

Flack pleaded not guilty to the assault charges and was released on bail. The trial was slated for March 2020. Flack's management were highly critical of the authorities for their dogged pursuit of her prosecution. They felt it was especially preposterous because the 'victim' Lewis Burton said he didn't want Caroline prosecuted. Burton was even still sending Flack affectionate messages on his social media. Flack's people seemed to suggest that the authorities were only making a big deal of this case because Flack was famous. It's hard to say if this was true or not. If you whack your sleeping boyfriend in the head you probably expect some sort of ticking off from the police. Whether it was grounds for a trial is open to question.

On the 15th of February 2020, Flack was found dead in her flat in Stoke Newington. She had hung herself at the age of forty. The stress of the media coverage and the prospect of an impending trial had all been too much for her. Stephen Teasdale, the father of a friend of Flack, had found the body after getting the keys from the landlord to see if Caroline was ok. Caroline's sister Jody was also there and tried CPR but it was too late. Flack was actually the fourth person connected to Love Island to commit suicide. This led to stories that the show was cursed. It was doubtless just a sad coincidence though.

Friends and relatives of Caroline later said her depression had been exacerbated not just by the authorities taking her to trial but also for what she saw as her abandonment by ITV after the case came to light. This latter criticism seemed a trifle unfair. ITV can hardly be blamed for suspending a presenter due in court for assault. They were probably planning to bring her back if she was found innocent. Sadly, that couldn't happen because she died before the trial could even take place

The friends and relatives of Flack were on firmer ground when they attacked the media and online idiots for making this period even more unpleasant and stressful for Caroline than it already was. Given that Flack was allegedly hyper sensitive to criticism and online abuse this was clearly a pretty awful time for her and one that she didn't enjoy at all. It was just a sad story all round. Caroline Flack was laid to rest at Greenacres at Colney, near Norwich. This was a ceremonial park set in a forest. It was a private service only for friends and family. The location was a beautiful resting place for a life cut tragically short.

ERIN FLEMING

Erin Fleming was born in New Liskeard, Ontario, Canada, in 1941. In the last years in the life of the legendary Groucho Marx, the much younger Erin Fleming became his secretary and moved into his Hollywood home. Fleming, who was a failed actress, clearly saw Groucho as her meal ticket and more or less became his manager. Her most prominent film role was a bit part in the 1972 Woody Allen movie Everything You Always Wanted to Know About Sex (But Were Afraid to Ask). Fleming only got a part in this film because Groucho was friends with Woody Allen and pulled a few strings. That same year Fleming had an uncredited bit part in Conquest of the Planet of the Apes.

Once she had wormed her way into the affections of Groucho (who was in his eighties now and rather doddery and confused), Fleming got him back on the stage, created Groucho merchandise, and acquired some Hollywood friends for herself. She even appeared on chat shows with Groucho.

Fleming liked to hint that she was in a sexual relationship with Groucho but this wasn't the case at all. Groucho just liked the companionship of a younger woman around the house. He actually encouraged Erin to find herself a boyfriend her own age.

Fleming proved to be a scheming and volatile presence in Groucho's life in the end. She did her best to turn Groucho against his family and clearly had designs on the inheritance of Groucho's estate. Fleming was a mentally unstable woman who used drugs in the house, would swim naked in view of Groucho's staff, and was even physically abusive to the elderly Groucho on occasion. To some Fleming was good for Groucho, providing companionship and getting him out and about again to meet new generations of young Marx Brothers fans who were thrilled to see this living legend in the flesh. But to most she was a shameless and scary gold digger taking advantage of an old man to secure her fame and fortune.

Groucho Marx died in 1977 and a legal battle between Fleming and Groucho's son Arthur Marx over the estate began. Arthur Marx eventually won his bitter duel with Fleming when Groucho's grandson Andy was appointed permanent conservator. Erin Fleming was sued for recovery of two houses, a Mercedes-Benz, municipal bonds and other gifts totalling more than $400,000 that she had received improperly. Fleming ended up with nothing and gave a frazzled and eccentric performance in court. After the court case, she was in and out of institutions and even had a spell on the streets as a homeless person.

Fleming spent the nineties in psychiatric hospitals and shot herself in 2003. She was 61 years-old at the time. Fleming's plan had obviously been to get sufficient control of Groucho in his last years so that she would inherit a generous portion of his money. When she ended up with nothing she was left with no plan B. Her acting career was finished (not that it ever started) and she had no way to support herself. Added to this was the fact that Fleming clearly suffered from mental health problems. As a consequence of this her last years were grim and difficult indeed.

IAN FLEMING

Born in London on May 28th, 1908, Ian Fleming attended Eton and Sandhurst but underachieved academically and failed the Foreign Office exams, eventually turning to journalism and joining the Reuters news agency in 1931. On assignment in Moscow, Fleming developed a fondness for vodka and caviar and established contacts with British intelligence. The seeds of James Bond were slowly starting to be sown. The young Fleming was a rather aimless and bohemian character for a time, wafting around the pre-war world on his travels with private money and becoming at one point 'the world's worst' stockbroker. But he quickly acquired the expensive tastes and habits that would play such a prominent role in the books that eventually made him famous.

During World War 2, Ian Fleming was in charge of 30 Assault Unit - a commando force that was deployed behind German lines. Fleming also advised the United States on setting up the OSS, the precursor to the CIA. By the end of the war, Ian Fleming was a Commander - just like James Bond. Fleming's most important relationship was with Anne, the wife of Viscount Rothermere. They lost a child together and then married a few years later, the marriage dulling the excitement of their formerly surreptitious liaisons

In 1952 he drew on his wartime experiences and began writing a spy novel called Casino Royale about a British secret agent called James Bond - the 'ordinary' name taken from the author of the book Field Guide to the Birds of the West Indies. On a bottle of gin a day at his GoldenEye retreat in Jamaica, where Noel Coward was his neighbour, Fleming rattled out the Bond books on his typewriter with their exotic mixture of sex and sadism in far flung places and elaborate journalistic detail soon attracting readers looking for escapist fare in the austerity of the era.

James Bond's famous request that his vodka martini be shaken and not stirred came from a theory Ian Fleming had that stirring alcoholic drinks somehow impaired the taste of them. Fleming yearned for critical and intellectual approval and the beginning of the James Bond series of films - with their glossy sheen and abundant technology - made him feel less likely to be taken seriously as a writer.

Ian Fleming initially hated the choice of Sean Connery to play James Bond. Fleming thought that Connery was too rough and not refined enough to play his hero. However, Fleming changed his mind when he saw Connery in action. The suave director Terence Young played a big role in the transformation of Connery. Young had his tailor cut sharp suits for Connery and taught him how to be more elegant and refined onscreen. Ian Fleming lived long enough to see Dr No and From Russia With Love made into movies but - sadly - he died just before the release of Goldfinger. Fleming therefore never quite got to experience the peak Bondmania that his famous character created in the 1960s with Goldfinger and Thunderball.

The James Bond movie franchise has tended to cherrypick titles, character names, and scenes from the Fleming books rather than adapt them wholesale. To give an example, the 1979 film Moonraker has little to do with Ian Fleming's 1955 novel of the same name - aside from the villain having the name Hugo Drax. The movie is about a villain who wants to create a new utopia in space whereas the book is about a secret government missile project on the Kent coast that James Bond has to investigate. Ian Fleming was a consultant on The Man From U.N.C.L.E. television spy action series from 1962 to 1963. Cubby Broccoli complained that Fleming was helping the opposition!

Ian Fleming's most experimental James Bond novel was The Spy Who Loved Me in 1962. This story is told first person by Vivienne Michel. Vivienne is closing down an empty hotel in the mountainous Adirondacks when two hoodlums turn up with orders to set the hotel on fire for the insurance. Vivienne is obviously someone these hoodlums need to eliminate to achieve their plan. She is saved though by the arrival of a mysterious stranger named James Bond. Fleming's The Spy Who Loved Me has almost nothing to do with the 1977 Roger Moore film of the same name. Fleming was unhappy with the book and stipulated that only the title could be used. One thing that does influence the movie though is Fleming's character Sol "Horror" Horowitz. Horowitz is a villain with steel-capped teeth. He was clearly the inspiration for Richard Kiel's Jaws in the 1977 movie.

The reflective tone that entered the later Bond novels echoed Fleming's own increasing sense of mortality. He drank too much and smoked too much and was far too fond of rich luxury foods, meats and butter, suffering increasing heart problems. Fleming's death was hastened by a complex and knotty court case he became embroiled in. Writer Jack Whittingham and maverick Irish film producer Kevin McClory both collaborated with Fleming on an aborted James Bond film in the fifties. The film never went into production but all hell broke loose when Fleming, in an act of incredible stupidity or incredible arrogance depending on your point of view, used the film screenplay as the basis for his Thunderball novel without telling Whittingham or McClory. The stress of the court case that followed is widely believed to have hurried Fleming to his grave from another heart attack and the victorious McClory was left with legal rights to make his own Bond film based on Thunderball.

McClory would be a thorn in the side of the Broccoli family for decades to come, infuriating them by making Never Say Never Again in 1983 and constantly threatening rival Bond projects or a 007 series of his own, triggering endless legal disputes. Even up to a few years before his death McClory was planning a new Bond film with Sony in the nineties, leading once again to more court battles with MGM and the Broccoli empire. Ian Fleming suffered his first heart attack in 1961 and never really recovered. On the 12th of August 1964, Fleming died of a heart attack he had suffered while visiting Canterbury in Kent. He was 56 years old. Fleming was buried in the churchyard of Sevenhampton, near Swindon. His last two James Bond books were published posthumously.

JOHN WAYNE GACY

John Wayne Gacy was born in Chicago in 1942. Gacy is one of the most evil serial killers in the history of the United States and given the competition that's really saying something. Gacy's childhood was unhappy by all accounts thanks to his strict father. He claimed too that he was molested as a child. Gacy worked as a mortician's assistant as a very young man and later seemed to confess that he had once fondled one of the corpses there. Although he had a wife and family, John Wayne Gacy was secretly gay. His family man image was useful though as a sort of disguise. When he got married, Gacy worked for a shoe company and was involved in The United States Junior Chamber (the Jaycees). This was a leadership training and civic organisation for people between the ages of 18 and 40.

As a young man, Gacy had worked as assistant precinct captain for a Democratic Party candidate in his neighborhood. The ability of serial killers to blend into society and appear normal is often called the mask of sanity. The mask worn by Gacy was very elaborate and convincing. He was once even introduced to the First Lady Rosalynn Carter at a function for the Democratic Party. Gacy changed occupations when he became the manager of a Kentucky Fried Chicken franchise. He was very successful in this and had a natural flair for business and promotion. However, the image he projected to the community as a generous family man and solid citizen was simply a facade. Gacy's secret life was dark and disturbing. In the late 1960s, Gacy sexually assaulted a fifteen year-old boy named Donald Vorhees. Gacy then gave another boy some money to beat up Vorhees so that he would be too intimidated to testify in a court.

The incident with Vorhees was far from isolated. Gacy had sexual relations with many teenagers and boys and he didn't really care about consent. Donald Vorhees refused to be intimidated though and told the police about Gacy. Gacy was sentenced to ten years in prison for underage sexual assault but he was such a model prisoner he was out on parole after a couple of years. The ability of Gacy to charm and fool the authorities into thinking he was a decent man was - tragically - something he would put into practice with his future victims. The authorities, sadly, seemed to somewhat lose track of Gacy after his release. He was able to go back into the community without it being public knowledge that he was a convicted sex offender. He lived with his mother for a while and then got engaged so that he could have have a new family. This new relationship gave Gacy two stepdaughters.

Gacy started a construction business and purchased a house in Norwood Park Township, an unincorporated area of Cook County. The address of John Wayne Gacy was 8213 W. Summerdale Ave. The construction business was a big success and made Gacy financially secure. Once again, Gacy was playing a role he loved - that of the solid citizen and pillar of the community. He was even dressing up as a clown to entertain the local children. John Wayne Gacy actually had two different personas when he dressed up as a clown. Sometimes he was Pogo the Clown and sometimes he was Patches the Clown. These two 'characters' had their own costume. It comes as no great surprise then to learn that Gacy would become forever known as The Clown Killer. From this point on he became one of the worst serial killers in history.

Gacy murdered 33 teenage boys and young men between 1972 and 1978. John Wayne Gacy's access to victims was provided by his construction business. He was constantly in contact with teenagers and young men looking for some temporary work. One of John Wayne Gacy's methods in getting his victims handcuffed was to pretend he was demonstrating a magic trick. He would escape from the handcuffs himself and then challenge the victim to do the same. Gacy would usually try and get his victims a bit drunk for this game. By the time they realised it was not a game and that Gacy was dangerous it was all too late. They were already helpless. John Wayne Gacy weighed 230 pounds. He was a big man who would have been difficult to fight off - especially if one was restrained.

John Wayne Gacy stuffed the bodies of most of his victims in the crawlspace of his home. When his wife asked about the smell he told her it was mice. Gacy used his experience as a mortician's assistant to block the cavities of his victims with rags and underwear. This prevented too much leakage after death. John Wayne Gacy would sometimes contact the police and report one of the men he had killed as missing. This was a tactic designed to make him seem trustworthy and throw the police off his scent.

Gacy drove a black Oldsmobile Delta 88. He liked this car because it had a big trunk. When his crawlspace started to get too full up with bodies, he used his car to throw dead victims off the I-55 bridge into the Des Plaines River. Gacy got divorced around this time and so had more privacy and time to himself - which was obviously a recipe for disaster when it comes serial killers. He was completely out of control. However, at long last, the authorities had finally started to take an interest in Gacy again.

A teenager named Robert Priest was reported missing and the police, upon further investigation, deduced that one of the last things Priest had done before he vanished was to visit John Wayne Gacy to talk about a job. The police, investigating Gacy further, now discovered the sexual assault conviction that had landed him in prison years ago. Further evidence against Gacy came from a young man named Jeffrey Rignal. The police learned that Rignal had accused Gacy of drugging and raping him.

The police decided to place Gacy under surveillance while they tried to build a case against him. John Wayne Gacy was very arrogant and full of bluster and bravado when he deduced that the police had him under surveillance. He liked to invite any detectives trailing him to breakfast. However, time was fast running out for this awful man. When the police obtained the legal right to search his house the game was finally up for Gacy. The crawlspace in his house was one of the most disturbing sights these detectives were ever likely to witness. Some of the bodies had become fused together in decomposition. Many of John Wayne Gacy's victims were found to have rope tied around their neck. It was an exceptionally complex and time consuming task to identify all of the victims. Sadly, to this day, there are still victims of Gacy yet to be identified.

Gacy was sentenced to death for the twelve counts of murder and spent fourteen years on Death Row. Gacy spent most of his time in prison painting. He liked to paint Elvis, Jesus, skulls, and Disney characters. Gacy naturally did a few self-portraits too - complete with clown costume. Gacy is said to have done 2,000 paintings while he was on Death Row. The Tatou Art Gallery in Beverly Hills tried to sell some of John Wayne Gacy's paintings. They were described as art brut. Legend has it that Johnny Depp owns one of Gacy's paintings. Two businessmen eventually purchased many of John Wayne Gacy's prison paintings in the end and had them destroyed in a mass bonfire where people (including relatives of Gacy's victims) gathered and cheered.

Gacy was killed by lethal injection in May, 1994. Gacy was allowed to have a last picnic with his family before his execution. For his last meal Gacy requested 12 fried shrimp, a bucket of original recipe KFC, french fries, and strawberries. John Wayne Gacy's last words before his execution were said to be - kiss my ass. He then taunted the police by saying they would never find all of the bodies. After his death, John Wayne Gacy's Pogo the Clown costume was put on display at the Alcatraz East crime museum. Gacy told the authorities that he had four personalities. The contractor, clown, politician, and then plain Jack Hanley. Jack Hanley, said Gacy, was the serial killer.

JAMES GANDOLFINI

James Gandolfini was born in New Jersey in 1961. He got into acting quite late after taking acting classes at 25. He had all manner of jobs before he became famous - including a stint as a nightclub bouncer. Gandolfini would appear in many films (The Last Boy Scout, Crimson Tide, True Romance, A Civil Action, Zero Dark Thirty etc) but it was the television show The Sopranos which made this actor immortal and world famous. The Sopranos ran for six seasons from 1999 to 2007 and ushered in a new era where television was a prestige event on par with film. Gandolfini portrayed the long suffering New Jersey Mafia boss Tony Soprano in the show and won many plaudits. It's fair to say that no one could have played Tony Soprano as perfectly and brilliantly as Gandolfini did.

On June the 19th, 2013, Gandolfini was in Rome enjoying a holiday. He was with his wife and young son Michael and due to accept an award in Italy as part of the trip. Gandolfini's parents were Italian immigrants so Italy was a very special country to the actor and somewhere he loved to visit when he got the chance. At around nine in the evening, Michael found Gandolfini passed out unconscious in the bathroom of their hotel room.

Michael called for help and an ambulance was summoned after hotel staff failed in their efforts to revive t+he actor. Gandolfini was taken to the Policlinico Umberto I hospital but died shortly after arriving. He was 51 years-old. James Gandolfini's cause of death was a massive heart-attack. It had been a sweltering day in Rome and Gandolfini had indulged in the local cuisine and booze that day by enjoying four shots of rum, two pina coladas, and two beers at dinner along with two orders of fried king prawns and a large portion of foie gras.

James Gandolfini hadn't looked especially well of late and if his last dinner was anything to go by he was clearly not adhering to the most healthy of lifestyles. There were stories before his death that he was struggling to control his drinking. He was alleged to have had battles with drugs in the past and perhaps the present too. The doctors spent forty minutes trying to save Gandolfini but it was all to no avail. The ambulance took around eight minutes to arrive after the medical emergency was declared. Gandolfini was pronounced dead at around ten-thirty. The U.S. Embassy in Rome was involved in arranging for Gandolfini's body to be flown back to the United States.

The actor's family and those that had worked with him were devastated by his death. It was a great loss to the acting world too because he still had many great roles ahead of him - which would now sadly never come to pass. A funeral service was held at the Cathedral Church of St. John the Divine in New York. It was attended by Sopranos cast members and many celebrities. James Gandolfini was then cremated and his ashes handed to the family. In 2021, Michael Gandolfini followed in his father's footsteps and played a young version of Tony Soprano in the prequel film The Many Saints of Newark.

PEACHES GELDOF

Peaches Honeyblossom Geldof was born in London in 1989. She was the second daughter of (the singer and Live Aid organiser) Bob Geldof and Paula Yates. Yates, a famous television presenter in Britain, died of a heroin overdose in 2000 at the age of 41. Peaches was sadly destined to follow in her mother's footsteps. Peaches went to a posh independent school and began writing for magazines and newspapers at a young age. She was by far the most high profile and extrovert of the Geldof brood and a presenter on many TV shows. Peaches was also a model. She was married twice at a young age and had two sons by the age of 25. In photographs of the Geldof clan, Peaches was always the only one not smiling. She liked to project a moody and aloof sort of image.

If you wanted to be very cynical you could say that Peaches was a hereditary celebrity. Examples of this 'showbusiness neoptism' would include people like Jaden Smith, Lily-Rose Depp, Brooklyn Beckham, and Kelly Osbourne. None of these people would be famous if it wasn't for the fact that their parents were famous. You could say the same of Peaches Geldof. It's hard to say what the actual specific talents of Peaches Geldof were but in her short life she was never off the television and a frequent fixture in the tabloids.

It's difficult to imagine that Peaches Geldof would have been writing for the Guardian, living in New York, flouncing around catwalks, and hosting endless television shows if she hadn't been the product of famous parents. She certainly took advantage of this though and seized fame by the lapels. Peaches was forthright, opinionated (or gobby if you prefer) and had a very high opinion of herself. Peaches took herself quite seriously. She had all the confidence and entitlement one might expect of someone who went to an exclusive school and grew up with a millionaire celebrity father.

Behind the scenes, there were always whispers about the private life of Peaches Geldof. In 2009 she was dropped by the underwear brand Ultimo after newspaper speculation alleging that she'd taken drugs. She denied the allegations and insisted this was just mistaken speculation. In 2008, Peaches had been questioned by the police after she was seen giving a drug dealer money. 2008 also saw the death of a friend of Peaches named Freddy McConnel from a drugs overdose. In his last diary entry he had written that Peaches Geldof was coming over later and that he planned to 'inject' for the first time. McConnel was just eighteen when he died.

The party lifestyle of Peaches Geldof seemed to come to an end though when she married for the second time and had two children. She lived in a house Wrotham, Kent at the foot of the North Downs. In an article, Peaches said that she was happier than ever and that married family life was bliss. However, Peaches had been taking methadone for some time and in 2014 fell off the wagon (so to speak) and died of a heroin overdose at her home.

Peaches was found by her husband Thomas after he became worried by the fact that she wasn't answering her phone. She was slumped over the bed when he found her. Thomas had been in London visiting his parents. It is believed that one of the two children was in the house in Kent with Peaches when she died but in another room. Bob Geldof was required to formally identify his daughter's body for the police. That must have been an unimaginably awful and sad experience.

Despite the spooky parallels with her equally doomed mother, the inquest judged that Peaches did not intentionally kill herself. She died of opioid intoxication and it was simply an accident. A quantity of heroin was found in the house and despite a police investigation it was never established who sold that heroin to Peaches. Her funeral service took place at at St Mary Magdalene and St Lawrence Church in Faversham, Kent. This is where she had been married and it was where her mother was married and had her funeral too. Bob Geldof owned a house in Faversham so Peaches had spent some of her youth here.

Celebrities who attended the funeral of Peaches Geldof included Sarah Ferguson, Jools Holland, Bill Wyman, Nick Grimshaw, Alexa Chung, Kate Moss, and Mariella Frostrup. Peaches Geldof was 25 at the time of her death. It was a devastating tragedy for her family. The house where Peaches died was virtually abandoned by the family after her death and left more or less as it was. No one could face even going there anymore because it just reminded them of Peaches.

JADE GOODY

Jade Goody was born in Essex in 1981. Her father and paternal grandfather had west Indian heritage and she suffered from some racism when she was younger - which was ironic given one of her later controversies. Goody had her first brush with showbusiness at the age of five when she made an uncredited appearance as a child extra in the ITV show London's Burning (this was a drama series about London firefighters). Goody became a dental nurse when she left school but she was destined to become probably the most famous reality television star in the history of British TV.

In 2002, the twenty year-old Jade Goody was a contestant on Channel 4's Big Brother 3. She lasted 64 days in the house and finished in fourth place. Goody was by far the biggest character on that year of the show and the person that everyone remembered the most. How much of this was completely unwitting though is certainly open to question. Jade didn't know how to be anything but herself. Goody was like the ultimate stereotype of the dumb Essex blonde. The fact that she was a bit dim made her funny and even sort of endearing. Jade Goody was like an enthusiastic puppy that just wanted to be loved.

Many contestants on Big Brother plunge back into obscurity once they leave the show but this certainly wasn't the case with Jade Goody. She went on to become one of the most famous people in Britain. Despite her image as someone who wasn't the sharpest knife in the drawer, Goody turned out to be a very shrewd businesswoman and self-publicist. The immediate years after Big Brother 3 saw Jade Goody make endless television appearances either as a guest or on other reality shows. She released her own fragrance (which was a big seller) and even brought out an autobiography. Jade Goody had essentially become a brand by this point. She was now a very famous and wealthy young woman.

In 2007, Goody was a contestant on Celebrity Big Brother 5. She entered the house with her mother and boyfriend Jack Tweed. Goody's decision to appear on this show proved to be her first major miscalculation since she had become famous.

Goody formed a little clique in the house with S Club singer Jo O'Meara and Danielle Lloyd (who was a model married to a footballer or something) and this catty trio seemed to develop a severe dislike for Shilpa Shetty. Shetty is an Indian actress who was also a contestant.

Anyway, Goody and her two co-horts were widely seen to be bullying Shetty and indulging in casual racism. The brand of Jade Goody, which had been so painstakingly built, took a severe dent as a consequence of this affair. Goody was so loathed now that there were no crowds when she was evicted from the house. An anti-bullying organisation dropped her as a patron. The person running Goody's career now was the (soon to be disgraced) publicist Max Clifford. Clifford's decision to book her on Celebrity Big Brother was, in hindsight, obviously a mistake.

Goody was even investigated by the police at one point for racism in the Big Brother house. She had to spend the following months doing the rounds of television studios making tearful apologies. Goody then brought out another fragrance. By now she had two sons with the presenter Jeff Brazier. In 2008, Goody agreed to appear on the Indian version of Big Brother. This was obviously calculated to make amends for the Shilpa Shetty affair and rehabilitate Goody's image and brand.

Two days into her stint on Big Boss (the Indian version of Big Brother), Goody received devastating news. She was told that she had cervical cancer. A tearful Goody had to leave the house and fly home for treatment. Despite the diagnosis, Goody continued to work. She appeared in a documentary reality show about her life, opened a beauty salon, and even appeared in a Christmas pantomime. By late 2008 though her cancer became more aggressive and she began losing her hair. Early in 2009, Goody's diagnosis was terminal.

Jade Goody got married to Jack Tweed (a magazine paid £700,000 for the rights to cover the wedding) and continued to receive medical treatment. Jade died on March the 22nd 2009. She was only 27 years-old. It felt surreal that someone so young and so famous could fall ill and die so quickly. Thousands of members of the public came out for Jade Goody's funeral. Even people who had never met Goody felt like they knew her. She was buried in her wedding dress in Epping Forest.

One positive to come out of this sad tale is that Jade Goody's high profile and openess in talking about her condition meant there was a surge in women coming forward for cervical-cancer screening. Jade Goody, through her fame, may well have saved some lives in that period when her own life was coming to a premature end.

OWEN HART

Owen Hart was born in Calgary, Alberta, Canada in 1968. Hart was a wrestler and had a long association with the WWF. He had various nicknames but was most commonly known as The Blue Blazer. The Blue Blazer was like a sort of comedy superhero character that Hart would play in the ring. Owen was the brother of Bret Hart and part of the Hart wrestling dynasty. Athletic and brave, Owen Hart was one of the best performers on the wrestling circuit and someone that that the company would always use in big pay-per-view events.

Away from the ring Owen Hart was married with two children. Other wrestlers would later say that Owen Hart was a very decent and well grounded man. He never fooled around with women or got into trouble. Once a show was over his only desire was to get back home to his family. Life on the road as a wrestler obviously involves an awful lot of travel and Owen found this the most difficult part of his profession. It was tough being away from home but the money was good so he had to make the most of it while he was still young enough.

On May the 23rd, 1999, Hart was in Kansas City, Missouri to

take part in a pay-per-view wrestling extravaganza. As part of the 'comedy' entrance for his wrestling character The Blue Blazer he was to be lowered into the ring in a cape by means of a harness. Once he reached the ring Hart was supposed to then trip over to comically deflate his character's elaborate entrance. Anyway, tragically, things did not go according to plan that night. It turned out to be just about the worst night in wrestling history.

As he got ready to be lowered, the harness release was accidentally activated and Hart fell nearly eighty foot from the overhead gantry. He land on the rope near a corner of the ring and then bounced off into the ring. Hart had initially landed on his chest and this caused internal bleeding and severed his aorta. The live paying audience at home didn't see the incident because a promo featuring Hart was playing for the broadcast at the time. As for those in the live audience, it was pretty dark when Owen fell so they (mercifully) didn't really see the accident either.

Those in the audience could plainly see that something had gone wrong in the aftermath though. Wrestlers are famed for their dangerous stunts but falling into the ring from eighty foot was clearly not a stunt. Something had gone terribly wrong. The stricken Hart was attended to in the ring and taken away on a stretcher. The pay-per-view commentators had to inform the viewers that this was not a storyline or part of the show. It was a dreadful ancient.

There was later contradictory evidence concerning Owen's attitude to the stunt. Some said he was perfectly relaxed about it and had done this sort of thing before. Others suggested though that he was nervous and unhappy about the stunt and didn't like the look of it at all. It is clearly evident that the safety precautions were lax. If you are going to lower someone into a ring from eighty feet you need to make sure there is zero chance of them falling or something going wrong. That obviously wasn't done.

Because of the internal bleeding, Owen Hart died only minutes after the accident. He was 34. What made his death even more sad was the fact that Owen Hart had been talking about life after wrestling in interviews. He said that when his contract was up he planned to retire and go and live with his family by a lake and take it easy. This would never happen now. The pay-per-view show that night carried on as normal after Owen Hart was taken away to hospital. This was seen as controversial in hindsight.

The Rock, who was wrestling that night, was told that Owen Hart had died two minutes before he went into the ring. He didn't much feel like going ahead with the show but he had no choice. The commentators announced to the television audience at home that Hart had died but the people in the arena were not told. Many were critical of the company for allowing Hart to do this stupid stunt in the first place.

The mitigation was that Owen Hart had done this type of stunt before. That was apparently with a different sort of harness though. The fateful night in question Hart was using a 'nautical clip'. It is believed that Hart might have unwittingly triggered the release of his harness when he was adjusting his cape. Owen Hart's family sued the WWF over his death and were awarded $18 million in compensation. They used this money to set up a foundation in his name. Owen Hart was laid to rest at Queen's Park Cemetery and Mausoleum in Calgary.

EDDIE HASSELL

Eddie Hassell was born in Texas in 1990. He got into show business because of his skateboarding skills. These skills earned him roles in commercials. Hassel also loved rodeo riding and surfing. He was the sort of actor who loved doing stunts. His first acting credit came in 2004 with the sitcom Oliver Beene. He was eventually best known for his roles in the 2010 Oscar-nominated film The Kids Are All Right and the NBC TV show Surface. In 2013, Hassell played the young Chris

Espinosa in Jobs - a film about Steve Jobs. His other television roles included Studio 60 on the Sunset Strip, Longmire, and Bones. Hassell was building a very nice little career in the acting world.

On the 1st of November, 2020, Hassell's life came to an abrupt and unexpected end when he was shot in Grand Prairie, Texas outside of his girlfriend's apartment. This incident happened in the early hours. Hassell was the victim of a carjacking that quickly turned violent. In contrast to car theft, carjacking is usually done in the presence and knowledge of the victim. Carjacking is obviously highly dangerous for the victim because the perpetrators of this crime tend to be armed and desperate.

It appears that Hassell was in no mood to hand over his car and things quickly got out of hand. Hassell was thirty years old at the time of his death. Eddie Hassell was shot in the stomach and died of his injuries before he could get hospital treatment. He had no chance of surviving a shot at such close range. An eighteen year-old Dallas teenager named D'Jon Antone was later arrested for Eddie Hassell's murder. D'Jon Antone shot Hassell and then drove off in the car he had stolen.

By all accounts, Antone was a well known local thief and robber and thankfully proved to be fairly easy for the police to catch - especially as they also had surveillance footage from the tragic incident in question. In a tribute on social media, Hassell's girlfriend wrote 'I'll see you on the other side of that skate barn in the sky, Cowboy. I'll always love you.'

Hassell's death came as a great shock to those who knew him and had worked with him. It was such a senseless and random sort of tragedy and this only made it even worse. What sort of person kills someone just to steal a car? D'Jon Antone was indicted on a capital murder charge. He is likely to have plenty of time to reflect on his awful crime in a prison cell for many decades to come.

CHRISTA HELM

Christa Helm was born Sandra Lynn Wohlfeil on November the 11th, 1949 in Milwaukee, Wisconsin. Helm was a bit part actress. Her roles included a small part in the TV show Wonder Woman. She was also in the 1974 horror film Legacy of Satan. Christina apparently had quite a tough childhood and suffered some abuse from the men who lived with her mother. She got pregnant when she was sixteen but the father (who was ten years older) didn't bother to stick around and accept any responsibility. Helm worked as a waitress in various places to make ends meet and nearly became a Playboy bunny at one point. A chance meeting with the singer and actor James Darren made her decide she wanted to be an actress. This ambition was modestly facilitated when she met costume designer Linny Barron.

Barron helped introduce Christa to some 'movers and shakers' and through a producer she started getting a few acting bit parts. Christa was the star of the 1974 low-budget action film Let's Go for Broke. This film didn't do much business though. Christa was dismayed when it didn't get a wide theatrical release. She inevitably moved to Los Angeles in the end and started living with a financier named Bernard Cornfeld in a plush mansion. Christa was, to put it mildy, known as a party girl. She would sleep with anyone - especially if she thought it might help her career. It is said that when she a waitress other waitresses used to warn her about taking home men she knew nothing about but Christa never paid much attention. Christa became notorious in Hollywood for her sexual exploits. Her conquests included many famous people - including Warren Beatty, Jack Nicholson, and Mick Jagger.

Christa apparently kept a diary which detailed all of her sexual encounters with the rich and famous. She considered this diary to be like a sort of pension or life insurance. It would make a juicy memoir or lucrative newspaper article one day. Christa is also alleged to have filmed some of her sexual encounters with the rich and famous just to make sure she had proof. There was later speculation had Christa plans to blackmail Hollywood bigwigs with her diaries and movies. Her friends are said to have warned her about speaking openly about this diary. They thought she was playing a dangerous game and would best advised to keep her mouth shut.

Despite all the Hollywood bed-hopping, Christa's career was still in no danger of taking off. She still hardly had any acting credits to her name. Her bit parts included a part as (appropriately enough) a waitress in Starsky & Hutch. Realising that her acting career had stalled and was going nowhere fast, Christa made plans to record a disco album but nothing much came of this either. It is said that she kept trying to sleep with her female backing singers. She was very ambitious and desperate to be famous but couldn't seem to find an outlet or opening for a career in Hollywood.

In 1976, Christa is said to have dated the permanently tanned and always dapper actor George Hamilton. She was also said to be involved with the disc jockey Frankie Crocker. Christa was also linked to actors and producers. She evidently still had hopes that her acting career might yet get a boost from one of these connections. For a time, Christa lived in a loft with a woman named Patty Collins. They were also lovers but those who knew Christa later said they felt that Patty was trouble. They detected a tension between the two women and said that Christa planned to end the friendship.

On the night of February the 12th, 1977, Christa went to a Hollywood party in Laurel Canyon with her roommate Stephanie. At some point, Christa left the party. She was later found stabbed to death outside of her agent Sandy Smith's house. She was 27 years-old (there's that old curse again - a LOT of famous people, if one could call Christa famous, have died at the age of 27). Christa was stabbed 23 times and also beaten with a heavy object. Sandy Smith was allegedly asleep and heard nothing. Christa's blood splattered body was found by a young man who walked through that street shortly after the murder.

The tyre marks and abrupt fashion in which Christa's car was parked that night led police to suspect that someone was following her and she was trying to get to Smith's house for safety. Residents of the street told police they heard what sounded like an argument coming from outside and then a scream. The knife which carried out the murder was never found. In fact, the case was never solved at all.

There wasn't much media coverage of Christa's murder at all. She wasn't famous enough to warrant much ink. As for suspects, well, they certainly exist. The agent Sandy Smith was later found to be telling an untruth when he said he was asleep as Christa was being stabbed outside his house. He actually had guests that night. What was he trying to hide by this lie? Those who knew Christa thought the prime suspect was her old flame Patsy Collins - who was a backup singer and lover to Christa.

The story goes that Patsy was furious when Christa went cool on her and said she wasn't even gay anyway. Patsy, according to this theory, stabbed Christa to death in revenge. Another suspect is Rudy Mozella - who was a keyboard player in Christa's disco band. She was hoarding some cocaine for him. The theory in this instance is that Christa used some of the cocaine herself and he murdered her as a consequence. Believe it or not, one of the people interviewed by the police in relation to this murder was Tony Sirico - who later became famous playing Paulie Walnuts in The Sopranos. Sirico was one of the last people to visit Christa before her death.

Christa's diary and tapes detailing her sexual encounters went missing after her death. This has obviously led to speculation that she was killed by some Hollywood figure who feared that she might release embarrassing scandalous information about him. The main suspect though is still generally judged to have been Patsy Collins. One of the main reasons for this is not just their storied history together but also because Patsy suspiciously vanished after the murder.

The police never spoke to Patsy Collins about this murder because they had had no idea where she was. Modern forensic testing on this case has suggested that Christa had female DNA under her nails when she died. This would obviously tally with the Patsy Collins theory. Christa's daughter Nicole continues to work towards some sort of belated resolution in this case. She hasn't given up trying to solve the riddle of her mother's awful murder.

MYRA HINDLEY

Ian Brady and Myra Hindley became known as The Moors Murderers for abducting and killing children on Saddleworth Moor between 1963 and 1965. The awful crimes shocked Britain and still haunt the city of Manchester. The Moors Murders shocked Britain most of all because a woman was involved. Myra Hindley was born in Manchester in 1942. She had a fairly bog standard background and became a clerk at an engineering firm when she left school.

In 1961, Hindley got a job as a typist at Millwards Merchandising. It was here that she met the vile and much older Ian Brady. Brady was a thief who loved reading Mein Kampf. Hindley was completely besotted with Brady and he would regale her with tales of the Marquis de Sade and Nazis. Hindley even stopped going to church because Brady told her that God didn't exist. The couple were soon planning bank robberies together and it's a great pity they didn't stick to that plan. What they did instead was indescribably evil and constituted the most harrowing crimes anyone could imagine.

In 1963 they abducted a sixteen year-old girl and murdered her. They then abducted twelve-year-old John Kilbride - who was raped by Brady and then had his throat slit before he was strangled. In 1964 they murdered twelve year-old Keith Bennett and ten-year-old Lesley Ann Downey. Lesley was forced to pose for nude photographs before she was killed. The evil duo would record the torture of the victims on audio tape and then bury the bodies on the bleak Saddleworth Moor. In 1965, Brady and Hindley killed seventeen year-old Edward Evans with an axe. However this death was witnessed by David Smith, the husband of Hindley's younger sister.

Smith called the police and Brady was arrested. It took a little longer for Hindley to be implicated in this awful case. The evil duo ludicrously tried to pin the murder on Smith but the police found considerable evidence which stated otherwise. They found tape recordings of victims, photographs of Lesley Ann Downey, and even a picture of Hindley posing on John Kilbride's grave. The trial took place in April 1965 and both Brady and Hindley were found guilty of murder and given a life sentence. They were both fortunate that the death penalty had only recently been outlawed in England.

The Moors Murders were incredibly harrowing and upsetting for the general public at the time. You could say that society was less innocent in the 1960s. Crimes like this were simply far less reported and less prevalent too. The thought that a woman was involved in the torture and murder of children was beyond belief to society at the time. Ian Brady said that as a boy on his paper round he encountered the face of Death - who showed him the vision of children on a moor. Brady, in his own mind, saw the Moors Murders as a sacrificial offering to the 'Death' figure who had visited him as a child. Brady's childhood 'vision' is probably explained by the fact that he had a form of epilepsy which left him prone to hallucinations.

Myra Hindley would later blame Brady for the murders and said that she was fearful of him and was abused. In cases like this it is fairly common for the female half of the duo to claim they were a victim too and had no choice. "I had this obsession about him," said Hindley of Brady. "This infatuation, I believed it to be love. I think it stemmed from the fact Brady was so different to anyone I had met. He seemed cloaked in an aura of mystery I could never quite penetrate, never quite solve and this unknowability intrigued me and continued to enhance his attraction to me."

Despite her expressions of remorse and attempts to get parole, no one really believed that Hindley was innocent and she will probably forever be the most infamous female figure in British true crime history. There were attempts, especially by Lord Longford, to release Myra Hindley from prison but the newspapers and British public were appalled by this. Hindley died in prison in 2002. Myra Hindley was still so despised that when she died the prison authorities struggled to find an undertaker willing to handle the cremation.

ADOLF HITLER

Adolf Hitler (1889–1945) was the dictator of Nazi Germany during the war and the man responsible for the conflict. He is remembered as one of the most evil men in history and was responsible for the deaths of millions. Hitler was Austrian but became a staunch German patriot. He served in World War I as a runner between trenches and also experienced life as an impoverished and failed artist. Hitler was left with a deep and enduring bitterness when Germany lost the First World War and - a bigot and racist - he also harboured a hatred of Jewish people (who he scapegoated for Germany's problems). It was a tragic and bewildering twist of history indeed that placed this highly dangerous man in charge of a powerful country like Germany.

After the war Hitler led the National Socialist German Workers Party and after years of struggle helped by the troubles of post-war Germany (which felt humiliated by the terms of her defeat in the war and had suffered from poverty and hyper-inflation) he became Chancellor in 1933. Despite vague early mumblings about working with other parties the Nazis soon exerted an iron grip on the country and Hitler began to plot expansionist policies based on his belief that Germany needed to right what he saw as the wrongs of the Versailles Treaty and secure "living space" for its people. What Hitler wanted was a German administered Europe that essentially existed as a Nazi Empire based on his racist ideology.

Hitler purged the army of some of the aristocratic Prussian officers who regarded him with suspicion and won over the generals he didn't dismiss by allowing them to proceed with new theories on tank warfare and boosting the strength and prestige of the army. The lightning campaign against Poland (without French intervention) made the initially dubious army look at Hitler in a new light. The campaign in the West saw France defeated in six weeks. Some generals had held doubts about the campaign but the victory seemed to justify Hitler's confidence and (erroneously as it turned out) the propaganda that lauded him as a military genius. A man whose own military career ended at the rank of corporal would end up commanding 300 divisions in battle.

After the Luftwaffe failed to gain the upper hand in the Battle of Britain, Hitler lost interest in an invasion of the United Kingdom and instead launched his ill-fated invasion of the Soviet Union. Hitler had an ideological hatred of the Soviet Union and regarded people in the East to be racially inferior.

Hitler believed if these vast lands in the East were conquered then German farmers and workers could settle there and Germany would be self-sufficient in food and oil. Hitler, swayed perhaps by the Red Army's poor performance in its war with Finland, believed that the Soviet Union would collapse in weeks if the German Army struck them with all their might. Despite the early successes of the campaign, Hitler's confidence turned out to be completely misplaced and, after the debacle at Stalingrad, Germany found itself fighting a costly war of attrition that it did not have the manpower or industrial resources to win.

Hitler's racial persecution saw an estimated 11 million people taken to concentration camps and murdered. In addition to the murder of Jews, Nazi Germany killed Slavs, Gypsies, gay people, and the disabled and mentally ill. Hitler placed the processing of these orders in the hands of powerful Nazis like

Himmler and Heydrich. As the war in the East rumbled on, Hitler spent more and more time at his military headquarters - the Wolfsschanze (the Wolf's Lair) in Rastenburg, East Prussia. Hitler was always far more interested in the war than German domestic politics.

He began to interfere more with the strategy and prosecution of the war, sacking generals and even putting himself in charge of the armed forces. While Churchill had Alan Brooke and Roosevelt had George Marshall as military chiefs who could advise them, Hitler would not appoint any equivalent figure. The most important figures in the OKW were Keitel and Jodl, two weak men who were loyal supporters of Hitler and loath to disagree with him. Keitel and Jodl were despised by the German military as yes men and lackeys.

When the Allied invasion of Normandy was successful and the Red Army launched Operation Bagration, it was clear that the war could not be won by Germany. It sounds ridiculous and simplistic but one of the principle reasons why Germany fought on was that it genuinely couldn't think of an alternative or anything else to do. The thought of surrendering to the Soviet Union terrified them for understandable reasons (especially once the vengeful Red Army had entered German soil and begun a bestial rampage of rape, murder and looting) and the Allied insistence on unconditional surrender allowed Hitler and Goebbels to claim that this would mean the end of Germany and would be unacceptable.

Hitler also believed that the alliance of nations threatening Germany's borders was one that could not possibly hold together. You had two very capitalist countries (Great Britain and United States) and a communist one (Soviet Union) so friction - in his view - was bound to occur. The Nazi high circle also clung to a belief and hope that Britain and the United States would eventually fall out and grow tired of their alliance. Nazi leaders could justify the continuance of the war on the grounds that if they just held out for long enough the coalition ranged against them would surely crumble and then the Americans or British might even join them in fighting the Soviet Union and protecting Europe from communism.

It was all nonsense but they clung to such unrealistic hopes when all seemed lost. This partly explains Hitler's Ardennes Offensive (aka The Battle of the Bulge) where he sacrificed Germany's last armoured reserves in a desperate surprise attack in the west through the Ardennes Forest. The aim of the offensive was to capture the port of Antwerp and split the American and British forces. Hitler believed that the Allies would argue and lose their appetite for war as a consequence and it would then allow him to transfer more men and tanks to the east where they were badly needed. But with the Wehrmacht lacking experienced battle hardened soldiers and desperately short of fuel for its tanks and vehicles, the offensive quickly petered out and fell hopelessly short of expectations. All it did was shorten the war because their armies in the west were now even weaker with the losses in men and tanks.

Hitler was surprisingly popular in Germany even up to 1944 and when he survived the attempt on his life by disgruntled army officers he even got something of a poll boost as many people were sympathetic and shocked that anyone would try to kill him. One other factor of course in Germany grimly holding out for so long was the belief that new "wonder weapons" would arrive to alter the tide of war in Germany's favour. People knew of the V rockets and jet-fighters. They wrongly assumed that Hitler had something even more amazing up his sleeve that he was waiting to unleash at the last minute. These mythical wonder weapons maintained some hope as the war came closer to home.

Near the end of the war, Hitler and his closest circle retreated to his claustrophobic, damp, but heavily fortified bunker in Berlin. The endless massed tanks and soldiers of the Red Army were within sight of Berlin with only some hopelessly outgunned and outnumbered German forces, including Hitler Youth, between them and the bunker. American troops were over the Elbe river and spearheads of Field Marshal Montgomery's 21st Army Group were closing in around Bremen and Hamburg. The French First Army was on the upper Danube and the Allied forces of Field Marshal Alexander in Italy had captured Bologna while General Patton's Third US Army raced south into Bavaria.

Hitler's bunker shook and rattled with dust as the shells and air raids continued from both the Allies and the Red Army. The war is lost but, trapped in this surreal atmosphere, Hitler fluctuated between rage and optimism. He gave operational orders to German Armies that actually ceased to exist weeks ago but still appear on his battle maps. Hitler was planning the defence of Berlin with phantom divisions. He was like a man playing a computer game. Nothing is real anymore.

In the last days of the war in Europe, Hitler studied development plans for his home town of Linz, oblivious to his plight. He devised a defence plan for Berlin and, with great enthusiasm, went over these plans with maps many times, talking out loud. General Walther Wenck's Twelfth Army and a rag-tag collection of units commanded by General Felix Steiner were ordered by Hitler to attack at two separate points against the Red Army and relieve Berlin.

In reality, Wenck's Army was defeated weeks ago and Steiner's forces were so weak, and his orders so ludicrous, he doesn't even bother to forward them to his men. When Hitler heard that his order to attack has been ignored by the generals he launched a furious tirade against them but finally realised the end had come. Hitler committed suicide on the 30th of April 1945 after marrying Eva Braun (who then killed herself with a cyanide capsule). Hitler shot himself with a Walther PPK - the gun later used by James Bond.

His body was the taken out into the bunker garden and burned - as per his instructions.

H.H. HOLMES

H. H. Holmes (born as Herman Webster Mudgett but better known as Henry Howard Holmes) was born in Gilmanton, New Hampshire in 1861. H.H. Holmes is often dubbed America's first serial killer. In the 1890s, he constructed a 'murder castle' above his drug store. This was a windowless room where he could torture and murder. The childhood of Holmes is somewhat vague in that there are conflicting reports of how bad it was or indeed wasn't. There seems to be no clear consensus.

Holmes attended various colleges as a teenager and got booted out of one of these schools for theft. In 1882 he entered University of Michigan's Department of Medicine and Surgery and managed to graduate in the end. Holmes later confessed to the murder of a medical school colleague as part of an insurance scam. By this time he had married and become a father - although he was said to treat his wife badly (he apparently even got married to another woman without bothering to get divorced) and they soon became estranged. Holmes moved to New York and there was a curious incident where he was seen with a little boy who then seemed to vanish. Holmes appeared to flee from the area before this matter could be investigated.

Holmes drifted around at this point and took a number of jobs. He was a compulsive fraudster and was also involved in the suspicious death of a boy at a drugstore. It was around this time that he changed his name to Henry Howard Holmes in an attempt to evade past deeds. In 1886 he arrived in Chicago and got a job in a drugstore - which he eventually purchased. He then bought a property across the road which he planned to turn into a drugstore and apartment building. There were even plans for it to serve as a hotel. The building was full of mazes and secret rooms and various 'chutes' and contraptions to dispose of bodies. Many women were seen going into the building but few came out again. Holmes tended to murder for financial gain and took out insurance on a number of victims.

The building was known as Holmes' Murder Castle. 'The first floor of the Castle had several stores,' wrote the Crime Museum. 'The two upper levels contained Holmes' office and over 100 rooms that were used as living quarters. Some of these rooms were soundproof and contained gas lines so that Holmes could asphyxiate his guests whenever he felt like it. Throughout the building, there were trap doors, peepholes, stairways that led nowhere, and chutes that led into the basement. The basement was designed as Holmes' own lab; it had a dissecting table, stretching rack, and crematory. Sometimes he would send the bodies down the chute, dissect them, strip them of the flesh and sell them as human skeleton models to medical schools. In other cases, he would choose to cremate or place the bodies into pits of acids.'

Holmes had an accomplice named Benjamin Piteze in his frauds and deadly deeds. The capture of H.H Holmes was rather knotty and slow. He was wanted for arson and so fled with the intention of creating another 'Murder Castle' elsewhere. He was eventually arrested in Boston in connection with a horse swindle. When the police investigated his Murder Castle they found a large number of bodies but decomposition made it difficult to say how many victims there were. Holmes confessed to over thirty murders but true figure is almost certainly considerably higher than that. He was an absolutely ruthless man who was perfectly willing to kill women, children, business associates, and generally anyone.

On May 7, 1896, Holmes was hanged at Moyamensing Prison. "I was born with the devil in me," he said. "I could not help the fact that I was a murderer, no more than the poet can help the inspiration to sing—I was born with the Evil One standing as my sponsor beside the bed where I was ushered into the world, and he has been with me since." There is a theory that H.H. Holmes could have been Jack the Ripper but the evidence is vague at best. The vast geographical distance between the two sets of murders alone makes it highly unlikely.

WHITNEY HOUSTON

Whitney Houston was born in Newark, New Jersey, in 1963. She was one of the biggest music stars in the world in her day and famed for her amazing voice. Houston's long list of awards and hit singles and albums was as long as your arm. She was a huge star and even appeared in the Kevin Costner movie The Bodyguard. Strangely enough, given all the things that happened to her in the end, Houston seemed quite clean cut when she first emerged in the 1980s. Houston was incredibly marketable, talented, and also a very beautiful woman. She seemed set to have a career that would last for many decades. Trouble was just around the corner though. Whitney Houston was soon to become what you might describe as a troubled sort of celebrity.

In 1989, Houston met the singer and songwriter Bobby Brown at a music awards ceremony. History would suggest that meeting Bobby Brown was the worst thing that could have happened to Whitney. They became a couple and got married in 1992. Their daughter Bobbi Kristina Brown was born in 1993. It is generally (though Bobby Brown would of course deny this) felt that a large portion of the blame for all the problems which Whitney Houston faced in her life from here on in (and even her premature death) must rest with Bobby Brown. Whitney's life seemed to become increasingly frazzled and eccentric once she hooked up with Brown.

Brown is believed to have introduced Houston to drugs and she was a hopeless addict for the rest of her life. She later admitted that Brown had given her pot laced with cocaine when they first became a couple. Houston, once the perfect music star, now started to look and sound somewhat addled. Sometimes she would seem thin and haggard - a far cry from the fresh faced Whitney Houston of the 1980s. There were stories that Houston smoked crack and whispers that the marriage with Bobby Brown was not only drug festooned but abusive too. You could see the drug mileage totting up in Whitney's face. She began to look tired. Whitney would seemed confused and not make sense in some of her interviews.

Houston and Brown eventually divorced in 2007. Whitney was given custody of their daughter. On February the 11th, 2021, Whitney Houston was found dead in the bath of her room at the Beverly Hilton in Los Angeles. She was 48 years-old. Paramedics tried to revive her when they arrived at around 3-30 in the afternoon but it was too late. Houston had been found by one of her assistants face down in the bathtub. No foul play was suspected or detected in this death and it wasn't a suicide. It was simply a strange accident - not helped of course by the fact that Whitney Houston was not exactly the most sober of stars.

Booze was apparent in Whitney's rooms and there was cocaine in her system. White folded up paper and a small spoon were found in Houston's hotel room. This was obviously being used to take cocaine. There were about a dozen prescription drugs in the room. These drugs had been prescribed by various different doctors. The battery of prescription drugs were not believed though to have play any role in Whitney's death. The general theory is that a drug and booze addled Whitney simply passed out in the bath.

A few days earlier, in one of her last public appearances, Whitney Houston had attended and watched rehearsals for a pre-Grammy Awards party. Those in attendance said that Whitney was acting very weird that day. She seemed very eccentric and full of manic energy. She also looked terrible by all accounts. The post-mortem revealed that Whitney Houston had dentures and wore a wig. Years of drug abuse had prematurely aged the singer. She was also suffering from early emphysema due to her heavy smoking. This is why she seemed to be slowly losing her beautiful singing voice.

According to the media, Bobby Brown was not welcomed at the funeral by Whitney Houston's relatives and had to leave early. After a star-studded funeral service, Whitney was laid to rest in Fairview Cemetery, New Jersey. In 2020, she was posthumously inducted into the Rock and Roll Hall of Fame. Whitney's $115-million estate was left to her daughter Bobbi Kristina Brown. The terms of the will stipulated that Bobbi would only inherit the full estate when was thirty years-old. There is a rather sad coda to this tale though because Whitney's daughter didn't live long enough to hit thirty.

In a spooky parallel with her mother, Bobbi Kristina Brown was found unconscious in a bathtub. She never recovered. Bobbi was 23 and died in Duluth, Georgia, in 2015. She was placed in a coma but died two days after she was found. Bobbi was a singer and actress and seemed to have a bright future. There was a lot of mystery surrounding Bobbi's death in that no explanation for why she had passed out in the bath was immediately forthcoming from the authorities. The Fulton County Medical Examiner's office later said though that Bobbi had marijuana, alcohol, a cocaine metabolite, and morphine in her system when she died. The official cause of death was cited as lobar pneumonia.

ROCK HUDSON

Rock Hudson was born in Winnetka, Illinois, in 1925. His real name was Roy Harold Scherer Jr. Rock Hudson was one of Hollywood's most beloved leading men in the 50s and 60s. Square-jawed, handsome, and 6'4, he was a major heartthrob. Magnificent Obsession put him on the map and he followed that with All That Heaven Allows and Giant (for which he received a nomination for the Academy Award for Best Actor). Hudson made dozens of films and was the classic all American leading man. He had longevity too. Right through the sixties and seventies he continued to appear in big movies. He is arguably best known for the romantic comedies he made with Doris Day.

In real life Hudson was also gay. Thankfully, it isn't much of a big deal today when a celebrity announces they are gay.

Hudson was less fortunate. He lived in an era when it DID matter. He had to go to great lengths to hide his sexuality for fear of it ruining his career. 'Nobody in their right mind came out,' said Lee Garlington, one of Rock Hudson's 'secret' boyfriends. 'It was career suicide. We all pretended to be straight. Once we met Paul Newman and his wife [Joanne Woodward] at a premiere. He looked at me and smiled. I just read in his face – that maybe he knew Rock and I were together. We kind of laughed about it.'

In 1955, Confidential magazine threatened to publish an exposé about Hudson's secret homosexual life. Hudson's agent Willson stalled this by disclosing information about two of his other clients. Hudson even married a woman named Phyllis Gates - who was his secretary - for a few years in the fifties to throw gossip hounds off the scent. Gates divorced him because he cheated on her with men. 'Lavender marriages' were a facet of Old Hollywood that seem preposterous today. A lavender marriage was where it would be arranged by the studio for a gay actor to marry a member of the opposite sex to quash rumours about their sexuality. The most famous example of this was Rock Hudson and Phyllis Gates.

It is often speculated that Danny Kaye's marriage to Sylvia Fine was a lavender marriage and it has been said that Barbara Stanwyck and Robert Taylor married each other to BOTH quash rumours about their sexuality. Not everyone was willing to go along with Hollywood's attempt to mask the private lives of the stars. William Haines, who is often referred to as Hollywood's first openly gay actor, ignored pressure from studios to enter in a lavender marriage in the 1930s and saw his career come to an abrupt halt as a consequence. Haines opened up an interior design business and got out of acting altogether because he refused to lie about who he really was.

The Disney child actor Tommy Kirk said that when the studio realised he was gay he was shunned by them. He ended up making beach party movies. Cary Grant is often alleged to have had a relationship with the actor Randolph Scott. Grant and Scott shared a house for ten years and would cook together, eat together, swim together, and give the impression of being a married couple. Grant and Scott were both in the film My Favourite Wife. Bert Granet, who worked on the script for that film, said that Grant and Scott didn't make any attempt to hide their close relationship.

By the 1980s, Rock Hudson began to work more in television as the movie roles dried up. He appeared some TV shows, TV movies, and television miniseries. In 1980 he appeared in an adaptation of Ray Bradbury's The Martian Chronicles. The last movie Hudson appeared in was The Ambassador. This was a 1984 thriller by low-budget rascals Cannon Films. Robert Mitchum, Donald Pleasance, and Ellen Burstyn were also in the cast.

In 1985, Hudson shocked fans and viewers when he appeared on television with Doris Day looking gaunt, emaciated and ill. His speech was slurred. Hudson announced that he had AIDS (which had only been discovered as a disease three years earlier by scientists) and died in October of that year at the age of 59. Hudson had travelled to Europe in the hope of finding a treatment but, sadly, in those days we knew a lot less about the condition than we do today. Hudson died in Los Angeles. He gave instructions that there was to be no funeral and that he was to be cremated after his death.

His last role was in the glossy soap opera Dynasty. There was some retrospective controversy about this because Hudson had kissed co-star Linda Evans in one scene despite knowing that he was HIV positive. There is salacious gossip that Hudson got AIDS from a male prostitute but others claim it was through bypass surgery. The high profile of Rock Hudson and the extensive coverage of his illness and death did at least have one positive benefit in that it made discussion of AIDS more open. It sort of gave the condition a public face. It also showed that anyone (even millionaire Hollywood actors) could get AIDS and so encouraged people to be more careful.

DAVID HUFFMAN

David Huffman was born in Berwyn, Illinois, in 1945. Huffman was an actor. He was married to the casting director Phyllis Huffman and had two sons. He got his start on Broadway and then moved into television. He appeared in shows like Lou Grant, Little House on the Prairie, Remington Steele, and Baretta. His film roles included parts in The Onion Field, the Clint Eastwood film Firefox, ice-skating drama Ice Castles, and the mildly cultish (if obscure) 1981 horror film Blood Beach. Though he wasn't a big star, Huffman was good looking and a competent actor. It seemed as if there was still plenty of untapped potential in his career. Fate was to intervene in cruel fashion though.

Away from acting, Huffman enjoyed sailing and painting. On February the 27th, 1985, Huffman was 39 years-old and appearing in an Of Mice and Men stage production in San Diego. During a visit to the theatre where he was due to perform in the play, Huffman noticed a Canadian tourist yell at a teenager who had broken into a nearby motor home. The motor home belonged to a couple the tourist in question was on vacation with. Huffman decided to apprehend the teenager. This decision would turn out to be a big mistake and have tragic consequences.

Huffman headed after the thief in his van before parking the vehicle and following the suspect on foot into Balboa Park. The actor managed to catch up with the thief in the park and it was here that things went terribly wrong. Huffman's attempt to make a citizen's arrest went tragically askew. There was a struggle and the teenager stabbed him in the chest five times with a screwdriver. Huffman died fairly instantly from these catastrophic injuries. The lesson from this awful case is that it is probably best to phone the police in situations like this. If someone is in danger or being attacked you would be be obliged to help them but chasing a criminal you know nothing about is probably not a great idea.

The killer of David Huffman turned out to be seventeen year-old Genaro Samano Villanueva. Villanueva was an illegal immigrant from Mexico. He was already a habitual thief and criminal and known to the police. It didn't take long for him to be brought into custody. Villanueva said he didn't mean to kill Huffman and had defended himself because he feared Huffman might hurt him. David Huffman's wife was less than impressed by this defence and argued that the killer of her beloved husband should receive the sternest possible sentence. Her wish was granted. On June 24, 1986, Villanueva was sentenced to 26 years to life in prison and admitted to the California State Prison, Centinela. David Huffman was laid to rest in Forest Lawn Memorial Park in Los Angeles. His life had been suddenly and shockingly cut short.

STEVE IRWIN

Steve Irwin was born in Victoria, Australia in 1962. He was a zookeeper, conservationist, television personality, wildlife expert, and environmentalist. Irwin became world famous for appearing in a host of animal themed television shows. Irwin loved animals from a young age and devoted his life to teaching us more about them. He was a natural performer on television with his cheerful personality and trademark khaki outfits. Irwin was sort of like a real life Crocidle Dundee. Irwin made cameos in Hollywood movies and was a frequent guest on the big American chat shows. Irwin's wife Terri was also involved in their shows and the couple had two children.

Irwin was building a huge franchise with his animal themed shows and documentaries. He was arguably (with the possible exception of Mel Gibson - who is billed as American anyway in most places) the most famous Australian person in the world by the time of his death. On September the 4th, 2006, the 44 year-old Irwin was shooting a documentary titled Ocean's Deadliest in Queensland. Irwin was fatally attacked by a stingray while shooting in the Great Barrier Reef. It was just a very unexpected attack that no one had forseen.

Fatal stings from these creatures are very rare. The stingray death of Steve Irwin was only the second recorded in Australian waters for over fifty years. The stinger penetrated Irwin's thoracic wall and pierced his heart. He had no chance of survival when this happened. The initial plan had been for Irwin to shoot a sequence involving a tiger shark but they couldn't find one so decided to shoot a short piece involving a stingray. This change of species unwittingly had tragic consequences.

Stingrays tend to be shy and elusive creatures so it was presumed that the stingray would simply get spooked and swim off when it saw Irwin in the water and they could capture this moment on film for the documentary. Sadly, that didn't turn to be what happened. The stingray struck Irwin multiple times in the chest. The cameraman only realised something was wrong when he saw swirls of blood begin to appear in the water. Irwin was still alive when they got him on dry land but he was in a bad way. The crew tried to stop the bleeding and implored him to hang on as they drove to a hospital. Irwin's last words were "I'm dying."

The footage involving the stingray attack on Irwin was later destroyed. It is speculated that the stingray might possibly have mistook Irwin for another undersea species and was attempting to feed. It was just terribly bad luck. Irwin's memorial service was viewed by 300 million people around the world and featured tributes from many celebrities and politicians. His wife described him as a cross between Indiana Jones and Tarzan. The Irwin family legacy lives on through his children - who both work with animals and so have continued the family's association with the animal kingdom.

There seems to be some mystery over where Steve Irwin was buried. It is assumed he was buried at his zoo because this is where a private service took place. His wife and children though have refused to confirm this and simply say that after his death they followed his instructions. There was some media speculation that Irwin had asked for his remains to be eaten by crocodiles in the event of his death. His family were quick to shoot this down though as a silly and rather tasteless piece of idle speculation.

MARTIN LUTHER KING JR

Martin Luther King, Jr was born on January 15, 1929 in Atlanta, GA. He attended Morehouse College and got a divinity degree from Crozer Seminary and then his doctor's degree in theology from Boston University. His father was a preacher and this inspired King to become a Baptist minister. King led the 1955 Montgomery Bus Boycott (inspired by Rosa Parks) and helped found the Southern Christian Leadership Conference (SCLC) in 1957. King wanted an America where there was no segregation and all people were equal. During the boycott, King was arrested and his house was attacked but he prevailed in the end.

In 1963, Martin Luther King, Jr. helped to organize the famous March on Washington. Over 250,000 people attended this march in an effort to show the importance of civil rights legislation. It was at this march that King made his iconic and famous I Have a Dream speech. The Civil Rights Act was passed a year later in 1964. King received the Nobel Peace Prize this same year. Tragically, Martin Luther King, Jr. was assassinated on April the 4th, 1968 in Memphis, TN. while standing on the balcony of his hotel.

King was shot in the neck. He still had a pulse though and was rushed to hospital. Sadly, the injury was too severe and he was pronounced dead. The person who fired the fatal shot was James Earl Ray - who had rented a room in a boarding house across the street from where King gave his last speech. Ray was a small time crook who had served time in prison. After the shooting Ray fled to Canada and somehow made his way to Europe. He was apprehended in London at Heathrow Airport and extradited back to the United States to face the music. It had taken a month to track down and arrest James Earl Ray.

There was no trial for Ray. He simply confessed his guilt and was sentenced to 99 years in prison. He later withdrew his confession and suggested a conspiracy was at play in King's death. Predictably though Ray had no evidence for any of these claims. There were though many conspiracy theories relating to this murder. The family of King actually believed that Ray was innocent and that some sort of conspiracy had been afoot. The conspiracies generally allege that Ray was a patsy and that army sharpshooters were there that day to make sure King was killed. Those who believe in this theory have argued that the gun Ray is alleged to have used did not match the bullet which killed King.

James Earl Ray died in 1998 at the age of 70. A crowd of 300,000 attended Martin Luther King, Jr's funeral. He is remembered not only as the unofficial leader of the civil rights struggle but as one of the greatest public speakers in history. His message of peace and harmony remains as vital today as it did during the fractious times he lived in.

SONNY LISTON

In the early 1960s, Charles 'Sonny' Liston was the most feared boxer in the world. Mike Tyson before Mike Tyson, but scarier. An ex-convict who was seemingly always in trouble with the law, Liston was linked to shadowy mob figures who still flitted around the boxing world at the time. When the uneducated, outwardly surly Liston blasted out liberal media darling Floyd Patterson in one round to become world heavyweight champion, no one - even black people - seemed very happy to have Sonny as champion. The hulking Liston was considered an unstoppable force but quickly lost his title to a gyrating young upstart named Cassius Clay/Muhammad Ali in two controversial fights. He faded from the mainstream boxing scene and was found dead in 1971 in very strange circumstances. Officially he died of a drug overdose but whispers in and around boxing often suggested there was much more to it.

Liston was always owned and controlled by someone throughout his life. Managers, mob figures, connected people, gamblers. Sonny was always caught up in forces beyond his control. Fittingly for the enigmatic Liston image, uncertainty always surrounded his place of birth and age. Liston said he was born in Little Rock, Arkansas, while a legal document once said he was born in Memphis. His mother said he was born in Forrest City while his managers said he was born in Pine Bluff. Liston's age was always a source of scrutiny and rumour when he was a boxer. He was always suspected of being older than he admitted.

The Listons were poor tenant farmers and children were told if they were old enough to come to the dinner table to eat they were old enough to work. "The only thing my old man gave me," Liston remembered. "Was a beating." At the age of thirteen Liston decided he'd had enough and ran away to St Louis where his mother and cousins lived. Liston turned to crime and ended up in 'Jeff City' prison - where he becomes a cult figure for standing up to white gangs who are picking on black prisoners. Not surprisingly, the formidable Liston's fistic potential is spotted by someone, in this case the prison chaplain Edward Schlattmann. Schlattmann was the first man ever to put gloves on Liston and remembered the boxer as a gentle giant.

When he was released from prison, Liston was now a boxer and a formidable one at that. "He hit me like nobody should be hit," said opponent Marty Marshall. "I was paralyzed. I just couldn't move." Liston was soon one of the most feared heavyweights in the world. When Liston was ready for a title shot the champion was Floyd Patterson. Patterson's shrewd manager/trainer Cus D'Amato (who later famously discovered and adopted a teenage Mike Tyson in the twilight of his life) avoided a Liston bout like the plague because he knew it was suicide for Floyd but Patterson (a sensitive and kind man outside the ring) eventually requested the fight and actually stood up for Liston.

Patterson asked for everyone to give Liston a chance and treat him with more respect. "Liston is as ill-mannered and insolent as a chain-gang boss," columnist Dan Parker says on the eve of their fight. Liston demolishes Patterson twice, neither fight going more than one round. Sonny is now public enemy number one. Even President Kennedy had told Patterson that he must beat Liston. Most people in America today would probably be hard pressed to even name a handful of active boxers but boxing, especially the heavyweight championship, was a much bigger deal back then. The heavyweight title also became entangled in the political strife and struggles present within America.

Patterson was intelligent, modest, polite, and didn't rock the boat. Liston was a monosyllabic scary looking ex-convict who was often in trouble with the police. It was simplified as the good black man against the threatening black man. When Liston flew home after winning the title he stepped off the plane to find not a single solitary soul was waiting to congratulate him. That's the way it always was for poor Sonny.

The monstrous Liston was considered to be unbeatable and his first challenger - an upstart by the name of Cassius Clay - was an 8 to 1 underdog and expected to slip into obscurity after the champion had inevitably exposed him. To the surprise of practically everyone, Ali (as he soon became known after converting to Islam) proved a far trickier puzzle to solve than Liston had expected and the champion retired on his stool after eight rounds. When Liston was stopped in the first round of their rematch by the so-called "phantom punch" (a chopping right hand thrown with little leverage close in) conspiracy theories were rife. Did Sonny throw the fight? We'll probably never know.

Sonny toiled away in the ring for several more years but his reputation was destroyed and although he racked up the wins no title shot ever came his way again. There was vague talk of a fight with Joe Frazier but this ended when Liston was stopped in the ninth by Leotis Martin. Liston might have been past his best by now but his brute strength and power was evident in his last ever contest when future world title challenger Chuck Wepner required 72 stitches after fighting Liston. Liston died in mysterious circumstances a few years later. It was officially a heroin overdose but everyone who knew him said he had a famous phobia about needles. Rumours say there was no dope in his system and it was all a plant to make it look like an overdose. If that is true who killed him and for what reason? The mob? It's a mystery that seems destined to never be solved.

DANNY LOCKIN

Danny Lockin was born in Hawaii in 1963. His family set up a dance studio and so Danny could dance almost as soon as he could walk. The family moved to California when he was young so a career in showbusiness was almost inevitable. Danny did some commercials as a kid. Trivia - he auditioned to be in The Sound of Music but didn't get a part. Lockin will forever be most associated with the musical Hello, Dolly! He played the role of Barnaby for several years on the stage and also in the film version with Barbara Streisand.

Despite this, Lockin's career never really hit the heights that he might have hoped for in the early days. He was very short and this made it more difficult for him to get acting roles. Lockin was about 5'6 so he was probably never going to be cast as the leading man in anything. Lockin was drinking a lot and using cocaine by the time he hit thirty. He must have felt as if his career was largely behind him now. Hollywood is littered with actors and performers who had a short prime and then struggled to get work after this. Lockin seemed to be another of those.

Though he had got married and had a son, Lockin was bisexual and starting to spend more time in the gay bars and clubs were were opening in California. In the end his wife left him, taking their son. Danny was devastated by this. By now he making ends meet by working in a dance studio. His dreams of Hollywood fame had vanished into the etha.

In 1977, Lockin made an appearance tap dancing on the crazy trashy TV talent series The Gong Show. It was to be his last performance. Lockin met his end after he went to a gay bar named The Mug in Garden Grove. He ended up going home with a 34 year-old man named Charles Leslie Hopkins. Though he had no way of knowing it, going home with Hopkins would be the biggest and last mistake that Lockin ever made in his life.

Hopkins lived at the modest Kona Palms Apartments in Anaheim and this is where they ended up. At some point the next morning Hopkins telephoned the police and said that a man had broken into his apartment and tried to rob him. When the police arrived they found the dead body of Danny Lockin. Lockin had been stabbed one hundred times. There were terrible stab wound injuries all over his body including his buttocks and back. It took two days before the body was identified. They managed to identify Danny by matching his fingerprints to prints the police had from when he was previously arrested for drunk driving.

The fatal stab wounds had been to the heart and lungs. Danny was 34 when he was murdered. Hopkins was clearly completely crazy. No sane person would be capable of such a brutal act. The police found a book in the apartment of Hopkins which was full of graphic depictions of men being tortured. They planned to use this as evidence that Hopkins had killed Lockin as part of a sick sexual fantasy. Now, you might well be thinking that this was a pretty open and shut case of murder. If you kill someone by stabbing them one hundred times in the United States you'd expect to get life in prison or maybe even the death penalty. To the dismay of Danny Lockin's family though this wasn't the case at all.

It was ruled at the trial that the torture book found in Hopkins apartment could not be mentioned nor used as evidence because the police who found it had not gained a legal search warrant. In 1978, Hopkins was convicted of voluntary manslaughter and sentenced to a three-year prison term. This was changed to four years and he was told with good behaviour he'd be out in two. Two years for brutally stabbing someone to death? It seemed to be a grave miscarriage of justice to say the least. Danny Lockin was interred at Westminster Memorial Park cemetery in Westminster, California. Hopkins died in 2006.

JAYNE MANSFIELD

Jayne Mansfield was born in Bryn Mawr, Pennsylvania, in 1933. A model, playboy girl, and actress, she was best known for her oversized chest and knack for self publicity. There was a time when studios looked to Mansfield to fill the void left by Marilyn Monroe's death but Mansfield didn't quite have Monroe's appeal and was certainly a lesser actress. Not that Jayne Mansfield let this get her down. She simply kept working - even if it meant having to do cheapie European pictures. Marilyn Monroe is said to have found Jayne Mansfield irritating and vulgar. She wasn't a fan. Marilyn thought that Jayne was a bargain basement impostor version of herself.

Mansfield is usually cited as the first mainstream actress to go nude in a movie. This was for the 1963 film Promises, Promises. She was simply very over the top and bold for the era. Mansfield was more than happy to flaunt her sex appeal and make as much money as possible from it. Jayne was sort of like a cross between Anna Nicole Smith and Diana Dors. She lived in a Hollywood mansion known as The Pink Palace which had a swimming pool shaped like a heart.

It's safe to say that Jayne Mansfield was a larger than life character. Despite her ditsy image (which she clearly played up), Mansfield was said to have a high IQ and play the violin. Jayne Mansfield was sort of like a character she invented to make money. You could say that Jayne was a very savvy and shrewd businesswoman.

On June the 29th, 1967, Jayne Mansfield's car crashed into the back of a tractor trailer on Highway 90 outside of Biloxi, Mississippi. At the time of the accident she had just made an appearance at a nightclub. Mansfield, along with two other passengers, Sam Brody and Ronnie Harrison, was killed instantly. Mercifully, her three children were seated in the back and survived the crash. The car had slid under the trailer - which tore off the top of the car. Mansfield, who was on her third marriage by now, was in a hurry that evening because she had to make an appointment to appear on television the next day.

Jayne Mansfield was 34 years old at the time of her death. Mansfield's acting career had never really taken off but she was still one of the most famous pin-ups of the era. It is sometimes reported that Mansfield was decapitated in the accident but this is not true. The car she was in did not see the tractor-trailer because of the haze of a mosquito fogger. It slammed into the vehicle and the front part of the car went under. The top part of Mansfield's skull was crushed. It could be that the decapitation myth came from the fact that some of Mansfield hair (or even wig) was visible on the ground in the aftermath of the crash.

Mansfield's death led to the National Highway Traffic Safety Administration requiring all semi truck trailers to be equipped with a DOT Bar. You may know it better by another name: the Mansfield Bar. A ghoulish note of trivia is that the car (a 1966 Buick Electra) Mansfield died in was later purchased by someone and became a tourist attraction. Jayne Mansfield's young daughter Mariska thankfully survived the tragic accident with just a scar. She is now an actress and has appeared in many TV shows - most prominently in the Law & Order franchise. Jayne was laid to rest at Fairview Cemetery, Pen Argyl, Northampton County, Pennsylvania.

JENNY MAXWELL

Jenny Maxwell was born in New York in 1941. Blonde and cute, Maxwell was a hip and in demand actress in the late 50s and 1960s. Maxwell was friends with the doomed Sharon Tate and said to like the party life. She appeared in big television shows like The Twilight Zone and Bonanza and with Elvis in Blue Hawaii. Maxwell was also in the 1963 film Take Her, She's Mine with Jimmy Stewart.

By the mid 1960s, Maxwell's star seemed to be on the wane. She had got divorced and lost custody of her son. She was broke and her career choices had become somewhat eccentric (she appeared in a strange film called Shotgun Wedding which was written by no lesser figure than Ed Wood). Her last acting credit was a 1968 appearance in the television show The Wild Wild West. Jenny evidently just seemed to lose interest in acting. Maybe the phone just stopped ringing and she couldn't be bothered with it anymore.

In 1970, Jenny Maxwell married Ervin M. Roeder. Roeder was a lawyer and twenty years older than Jenny. It has been suggested that Jenny married Roeder because she wanted some security and stability in her life now that her acting career was history. Ervin was pretty rich so she wouldn't have to worry about money so long as he was her husband. Roeder had connections in Hollywood and was said to be something of a blowhard who liked to give the impression he had mob connections.

The marriage between Maxwell and Roeder became very tense in the end. They both had affairs and Roeder was said to have become increasingly bitter at the thought of Jenny Jenny Maxwell inheriting all of his money should he shuffle off this mortal coil before her (which seemed more than likely given that she was much younger than him). Maxwell is alleged to have wanted to leave Roeder but clung onto the marriage because her lawyer told her that she would get a bigger divorce settlement if she was married past ten years.

On June the 10th, 1981, the couple were together in Beverly Hills because Roeder had offered Jenny a lift home after she visited a hospital for minor treatment. By now they were not living together but still on fairly civil terms. In the lobby of Maxwell's Beverly Hills condo that afternoon they were both shot and killed. Jenny was shot in the head while Roeder was shot in the abdomen. It was a puzzling double murder which was never officially solved. Jenny Maxwell was 39 years-old when her life came to this gruesome and sudden end. It was a mystery to the police why anyone would want to kill a former actress and her lawyer husband.

Years later a theory on the murder surfaced. The theory alleges that Roeder hired a hitman to kill Jenny that afternoon so he wouldn't have to pay spousal support. The hitman was, according to his theory, told to make it look real and so fire a shot at Roeder too or maybe give him a non lethal injury. The hitman, if this theory is true, was obviously not a very good shot! The hitman ended up killing the person who had hired him to kill his wife!

A weird detail in this case is that because Jenny was killed first in the lobby her estate legally transferred to her husband. When he died straight after, Roeder's children became the heirs to Jenny's estate. Jenny's son from her first marriage didn't get a penny. I'd imagine Jenny's son was quite bitter about that. I know I would be. Jenny Maxwell was later cremated and her ashes scattered at sea.

FREDDIE MILLS

Freddie Mills was a famous and popular British boxer who won the world light-heavyweight championship against Gus Lesnevich in 1948. After he retired from boxing, Mills became an actor and appeared in a slew of British films in the 50s and 60s - including two Carry On films. In 1965, the 46 year-old Mills was found dead in his car in London from a gunshot wound. The coroner judged that the death was a suicide. Mills had left his nightclub to take a nap in his car (which he often did) and then shot himself with a rifle. It was presumed to be a murder at first but then judged a suicide.

Mills was said to be depressed at the time of his death because of a debt he owed to some gangsters. A number of bad business ventures had left Mills in financial trouble. Mills made a fortune from his boxing career but only had £387 to his name when he died. His apparent suicide was a great shock because he always seemed such a cheerful and popular character. In more recent years a rather outlanish conspiracy theory has surfaced which contends that Mills was actually a serial killer!

Hammersmith in London was the scene of a number of grisly murders in 1964 and 1965. The killer became known as Jack the Stripper because the murder victims were all prostitutes and always had their clothes and belongings (including, believe it or not, false teeth) removed. However, despite a huge police operation, the killer was never found and the murders remain a mystery to this day. The puzzling thing about the murders is that none of the victims displayed any evidence of sexual violence. The police detective heading up the search for Jack the Stripper in the 1960s predicted that the case would be as famous as the Jack the Ripper murders. He was obviously completely wrong about that. A lot of people today seem to have barely heard of Jack the Stripper.

The victims were nearly all in their twenties and are believed to have been killed in private before their bodies were dumped in a public place. Chief Superintendent John Du Rose was in charge of the investigation for Scotland Yard and had six-hundred police officers involved in the search for Jack the Stripper. They set up observation posts in a 24 square mile area of London and questioned thousands of potential suspects and yet - remarkably - they never found the killer. So who was Jack the Stripper?

At one point the police seemed to make a breakthrough when

analysis of paint particles suggested the victims had been stored at an abandoned factory on the Heron Trading Estate.

The police therefore began questioning hundreds of workers on the estate. A man named Mungo Ireland was heavily suspected by the police at one point because he'd worked as a security guard at the estate but Ireland was proven to have been in Scotland when one of the murders took place and was removed from the list of suspects.

One of the prostitute victims of Jack the Stripper had been seen getting into a car with two men before her death but the police could never find these two men or the car in question. This lead though did seem to suggest it wasn't impossible that Jack the Stripper was two men rather than one. Another suspect in the case was an embittered former police detective who lived in the area and had been caught committing burglaries in an attempt to embarrass the police. However, this man could not be linked to the Stripper murders and so was eventually removed from the list of potential suspects.

One of the more bizarre theories (which has even been the basis of a book) is that the killer was Freddie Mills. The notion that Freddie Mills was Jack the Stripper might have started with the gangster Frankie Fraser. The word of Frankie Fraser is not exactly the most empirical evidence. Fraser supposedly said it to policeman Bob Berry, who told The Sun crime reporter Michael Litchfield. Litchfield subsequently wrote a book called The Secret Life of Freddie Mills. Litchfield claims Mills was a mason and confessed the murders to Scotland Yard Chief Superintendent John Du Rose. It should be stressed that the detective in charge of the case, Nipper Read, dismissed Freddie Mills as a suspect.

The police officers involved in this case suspected that because Mungo Ireland was also a former boxer some wires might have been crossed somewhere along the line which dragged Freddie Mills (with the aid of some gangster whispers and tittle-tattle) in the game of Stripper suspects bingo. It is possible (if doubtful) that the real Jack the Stripper might even still be alive today. It is certainly plausible that if Jack the Stripper had been captured the killer would be as famous as British serial killers like Peter Sutcliffe or Dennis Nilsen today. Surprisingly, this killer remains little known - perhaps as a consequence of the fact that he was never caught. He did though at least leave one lasting legacy. The classic Alfred Hitchcock film Frenzy was heavily inspired by the Jack the Stripper murders.

There has been much conjecture about the death of Freddie Mills and whether or not it was really a suicide. There is certainly some element of doubt but because it was so long ago now and principle figures and police officers from that era are mostly no longer around it is hard to say if the real truth will ever come out. There are theories that Mills was murdered by a mobster or an embittered former boxing manager but we simply don't know if any of these theories are true.

ASHLEIGH ASTON MOORE

Ashleigh Aston Moore was born in Sunnyvale, California, in 1981. She started appearing in commercials at the age of four. Her big break was landing the dual roles of Alpha and Donna in the CBC Television children's series The Odyssey in 1992. She appeared in a couple of TV movies and then had her most famous part as Chrissy in the 1995 film Now and Then. Though this film got middling reviews it seems to be mildly cultish these days. Ashleigh starred with Christina Ricci, Thora Birch, and Gaby Hoffmann as younger versions of characters in the film. Ashleigh played the younger version of Rita Wilson. The same year as this movie came out Ashleigh made an appearance in the popular television show Northern Exposure.

Now and Then (for which she won a YTV Achievement Award) could potentially have been a star making role for Ashleigh Aston Moore but, as often happens in Hollywood, things did not quite go according to plan. She made a couple more (now forgotten) movies and then appeared in a television film. Her last credit was an episode of Touched By An Angel in 1997. After that Ashleigh drifted out of acting and vanished into obscurity. She attended East Carolina University and appeared in some student films there. Sadly, once she left college Ashleigh seemed to lose any sense of direction.

In 2007, Ashleigh Aston Moore died of a heroin overdose at the age of 26. It seems that Moore, like a number of child stars who have fallen on hard times, tried to use drugs to fill the hole left by the loss of fame and an acting career. "Ashleigh was a really cool kid," her Now and Then co-star Thora Birch said in 2015. "She had a great personality and I remember making fun of 'Chrissy's' lines with her from time-to-time because neither of us could believe that Chrissy was so clueless. I had not heard about her passing until a couple years ago, and was saddened by the news. She still lives on as Chrissy to me, though."

Ashleigh was suffering from pneumonia and bronchitis at the time of her death and in poor health. She also allegedly suffered from lupus. Moore was estranged from her family when she died. It is said that she got hooked on heroin as a teenager but had been clean for a number of years before a relapse. At the time of her death she was emaciated and covered in tattoos and piercings. She was unrecognisable from that little kid in Now and Then. Ashleigh didn't need to work because she still earned decent royalties from her acting career. This was a recipe for disaster in many ways because it gave her plenty of spare time and also the funds to buy drugs. A deadly combination.

At the time of her death, Ahleigh had apparently just done a voice role for the HBO educational series Lulu's World. It seems plausible that if she had got clean she could have staged an acting comeback. Stars like Robert Downey and Drew Barrymore have been through drugs problems and come out the other side. Alas though it wasn't to be the case for Ashleigh

Aston Moore. After her death she was cremated and her ashes were handed to her family. It is not known where the ashes were scattered or buried.

TOMMY MORRISON

When Sylvester Stallone was looking for a young actor to play Rocky Balboa's protege in the 1990 sequel Rocky V he decided it would be a good idea to hire someone who was a real boxer. Stallone had tried to do this in the original Rocky when Ken Norton (an active world ranked heavyweight at the time) was cast as Apollo Creed. Norton bailed out at the last minute and was replaced by Carl Weathers. Years later Stallone would hire former world champion boxer Antonio Tarver to play Rocky's opponent in Rocky Balboa.

The fifth go around brought back the original Rocky director John G Avildsen in an attempt to go back to basics and make a more grounded sort of Rocky film more in line with the first one. The film has Rocky back from Russia after his fight with Ivan Drago. Life turns sour for our hero when he learns his brother-in-law Paulie (Burt Young) has frittered his fortune away on a bad real estate deal. Rocky is bankrupt but can't box anymore because of brain damage he suffered in his career. Rocky is forced to move back to his old neighbourhood and Adrian (Talia Shire) gets her old pet shop job again. Rocky finds a new purpose in life though when he takes a young fighter named Tommy Gunn under his wing.

Stallone's people left no stone unturned looking for someone to play Tommy Gunn and came up with what appeared to be the perfect candidate. Tommy Morrison was a real life 21 year-old heavyweight prospect from Arkansas. Morrison was 6'2, muscled, a puncher (famed for his deadly left-hook) with a crowd pleasing style, blonde, good looking, and articulate. Morrison's handlers even came up with a great marketing gimmick by (dubiously) claiming he was related to John Wayne - thus earning him his nickname 'Duke'. Morrison was cast as Tommy Gunn and saw his profile go through the roof. Stallone even shot footage at some of Morrison's real fights to use in Rocky V.

Morrison loved making Rocky V and said it was a great experience. His plan was to become the world heavyweight champion and then once his boxing career had run its course he would go back to acting again. Sadly, Morrison's plans never came to fruition on either of those two fronts. Morrison was passable enough in Rocky V. He's obviously more convincing in the boxing scenes than he is with dialogue (especially when Stallone's script abruptly - and not entirely convincingly - turns Tommy Gunn into an angry villain who hates Rocky and wants to go off with some Don King style loudmouth) but he had the potential to get better and do more movies.

As far as his real boxing career went, despite a devastating loss to Ray Mercer, Morrison seemed to have reached the summit - or at least the top part of the mountain - when he decisioned the ageing but still formidable icon George Foreman in 1993. Morrison showed surprising boxing skills that night and jabbed his way to victory over his lethal but lumbering opponent. However, Morrison was never the most stable person outside the ring and was never able to capitalise on the Foreman fight. Outside the ring he loved the party lifestyle and drank too much. He was a notorious womaniser and very promiscuous. His team were also dismayed by the fact that Morrison continued to take banned steroids.

Morrison blew a multi-million dollar payday with Lennox Lewis when he was stopped in one round by the unheralded Michael Bent. Morrison said he simply hadn't trained or prepared properly for Bent. The fight with Lewis still happened but Morrison had to take a much lower purse due to the commercial damage done to his 'brand' by the Bent loss. Morrison was soundly beaten by the formidable Lewis and took a lot of punishment before the fight was stopped in the sixth round. Despite the losses, Morrison was still marketable because he was white (although he also had Native Indian ancestry) and a puncher.

Morrison signed a deal with Don King (which was rather ironic because the sleazy motor mouthed promoter George Washington Duke in Rocky V is patently based on Don King!) and prepared for a comeback fight. Mike Tyson was out of prison by now and King had promised Morrison that if he won his next fight he would fight Mike Tyson next. Tyson v Morrison, a battle of two big punchers who both come forward, was sure to land Tommy Morrison a very sizeable purse. Not only that, but Morrison was convinced he could win the fight.

Before this could happen though, Morrison was diagnosed with AIDS and had to retire from boxing. The diagnosis, from a pre-fight medical, came only hours before he was due in the ring. "I lived a permissive, fast and reckless lifestyle," said Morrison. "I hope I can serve as a warning that living this lifestyle can really lead to only one thing and that's misery. . . . I've never been so stupid in my life. I thought I was bulletproof and I'm not. If getting up here and confronting this problem out in the open can get just one person out there to take a more responsible attitude toward sex, then I would feel I scored my biggest knockout ever."

Despite these wise words, Morrison would gradually start to become detached from reality in the years that followed. He stopped taking his AIDS medication and started to insist that the HIV tests had been false. A very conservative Christian, Morrison came to believe that only gay men could get AIDS. In the throes of these dangerous delusions, Morrison's health started to suffer. He began having pectoral implants and continued taking steroids to try to maintain his physique. He ended up looking grotesque - with stick thin arms and a HGH gut. Morrison ended up looking like a shadow of the handsome Tommy Gunn character he played in Rocky V. He now looked like a dishevelled old man.

Morrison's inability to stay out of trouble with the law was also beginning to escalate. He had various charges for drunk driving, firearms possession, and drugs. In 2000 he was sentenced to two years in prison. In 2007, Morrison returned to the boxing ring at Mountaineer Casino Racetrack and Resort, Chester, West Virginia. Morrison had to shop around for a state with less than stringent medical rules and fought an inactive journeyman named John Castle. Morrison looked pitiful but won the fight in the second round.

A year later, Morrison fought an equally meaningless and equally rigged looking bout against Matt Weishaar in Mexico. It was a sad sight watching this once spectacular heavyweight plodding around looking emaciated, fighting in front of a sparse crowd for peanuts. Morrison was so desperate for money he took to staging 'mixed martial arts' fights in nightclubs. In 2011, Morrison tried to fight again under the auspices of the Quebec Boxing and Gaming Commission but refused to take a HIV test. He said he didn't trust athletic commission tests. In 2013, Morrison's health began to fail him. He contracted Guillain-Barré Syndrome and became bed bound - an emaciated shadow of the powerful athlete he had once been. His mother said they were simply waiting for him to die although Morrison's current wife Trisha still insisted that he didn't have HIV.

On September the 1st, 2013, Morrison died at the Nebraska Medical Center in Omaha, Nebraska at the age of 44. According to the Nebraska Department of Health & Human Services, Morrison's cause of death was cardiac arrest, resulting from multiorgan failure due to septic shock caused by a Pseudomonas aeruginosa infection. Morrison's story was a sad case of someone who once had everything ending up with nothing. It was also a tragically self-destructive tale. If Morrison had taken his HIV medication and listened to his doctors he would probably still be alive today with a condition that no longer has to be a death sentence.

ENRIQUETA MARTI

Enriqueta Martí was born in Catalonia in 1868. As a young woman she moved to Barcelona and became a prostitute. She is said to have got married but this was apparently a stormy affair that didn't last very long. Enriqueta Martí opened her own brothel but found that some of the clients there had particular (not to mention criminal) tastes and liked young children. Enriqueta Martí therefore began abducting children so she could 'pimp' them in her brothel to paedophiles.

As if that wasn't bad enough, Martí was also killing them to make all manner of creams and potions in her self-styled role as a mystical guru and witch-doctor. Enriqueta Martí is even said to have drank the blood of her child victims because she believed drinking blood cured medical ailments and kept one healthy. Martí was arrested in 1909 when it came to light she used children in her brothel but she escaped any serious charges and was not punished for these crimes. It is assumed that because some police officers used the brothel, Martí was able to use this information to get herself off the hook.

Her activities, all told, went on for some time and more children were inevitably abducted after her close brush with the law. She was finally arrested in 1912. It is claimed she was caught when a little girl at the brothel went to a window and was seen by someone outside. Enriqueta Martí always told the abducted children to stay away from the windows. The police found two little girls in the brothel and Enriqueta Martí (rather unconvincingly) told them that one girl was her daughter and another was an orphan she was looking after.

'The girls told the police that their captor would only feed them potatoes and bread,' wrote STSTW Media. 'She would pinch them if they misbehaved such as going to the windows, balconies or other rooms. Those other rooms told a story even darker than kidnapping. The girls were first to explore them in their bored isolation beforehand and so guided the police inside. There they found bloody clothes and a myriad of evidence to incarcerate the supposed vampiress. Thirty small bones, many of which exposed to fire was one such proof. There were many jars with strange remains, blood, bones and hair. There were clothes covered in blood, knives and bones. Angelita also spoke of a young boy called Pepito who she witnessed being killed by a knife on the kitchen table by Martí.'

The police are said to have found hidden walls in the brothel which contained the grisly potions (said to be popular with the elites of Barcelona because Enriqueta Martí told them they cured tuberculosis) and alleged human bones. Enriqueta Martí didn't really offer a confession in the end. She said she was responsible for the unusual potions but never admitted to killing anyone. She also refused to reveal the names of clients who used her brothel and purchased her potions. Enriqueta Martí was never actually tried in the end. She was taken into custody and died just over a year later when other prisoners beat her to death. Martí is naturally known as The Vampire of Barcelona in crime articles today.

The story of Enriqueta Martí is strange and grisly indeed but not believed by everyone. Some writers believe she was made a scapegoat for the fact that the police were struggling to solve a rash of child abductions in the area. There appears to be enough evidence though to suggest that, at the very least, Enriqueta Martí was a sinister and dangerous character with a rather dodgy and wayward moral compass.

BENITO MUSSOLINI

Benito Mussolini (1883–1945) was the dictator of Italy for most of the war. Italy joined Nazi Germany and Japan to become known as the Axis Powers. He ruled Italy from 1922 until he was deposed in 1943. He later became the leader of the Italian Social Republic (a Nazi puppet regime in the north of Italy) after he was rescued by German special forces. Mussolini moved fast to create a totalitarian state in the early days and managed to gain complete control of the country.

Known as Il Duce ("the leader"), Mussolini was pompous and arrogant and the poor performance of the Italian armed forces in World War 2 never gave him an especially strong hand to play in his meetings with Hitler.

Mussolini threw Italy behind Hitler's Germany in the war as he was sure that the Nazis would dominate Europe and successfully invade Great Britain. Mussolini had a particular dislike of Britain and wanted the Royal Navy's dominance of the Mediterranean ended. Although the Italian Army was nowhere near as modern, formidable, powerful and professional as the German one, Mussolini believed that they had to show a willingness to fight and make sacrifices to get a jackal's share of the bounty in the new Nazi Europe that was coming. Unfortunately for Mussolini this led to no small degree of humiliation when the Italian campaigns in Greece and North Africa were unsuccessful and Hitler had to dispatch German troops to help them.

The eventual Axis collapse in North Africa had profound consequences for Italy because it meant they were the next target for the Allies. Mussolini had also committed an Italian army of 235,000 soldiers to fight alongside the Germans in the Soviet Union but the army was eventually destroyed there with only the remnants returning home. With Italy tired of war and military disasters and aware that the Axis now looked like the losing side, Mussolini was deposed by King Victor Emmanuel III in 1943 but rescued by Otto Skorzeny on the orders of Hitler and smuggled to Germany.

The war had gone sour for Italy and everyone was aware the Allies were on the way to victory. Italy was more or less a puppet state run by Germany and Mussolini was bitter and frustrated. He wrote his memoirs and tried to shift the blame for the disasters and humiliations heaped upon the Italian armed forces in the war onto others. In April 1945, with defeat closer than ever, Mussolini fled north but was captured by partisans. He was killed and his body - alongside that of his mistress - was taken to Milan and hung for the public to see.

The dictator and his mistress were hung up at a petrol station and mutilated. When Hitler heard of this it strengthened his resolve not to be captured alive.

DENNIS NILSEN

Dennis Andrew Nilsen was born in 1945 in Fraserburgh, Aberdeenshire, Scotland. Nilsen is one of the worst serial killers in British history. Nilsen eventually confessed to murdering fifteen men and said he tried to kill others. His spree took place from 1978 to 1983. Dennis Nilsen's confirmed verified victims are Kenneth Ockenden, Martyn Duffey, William Sutherland, Stephen Holmes, Malcolm Barlow, John Howlett and Stephen Sinclair. The victims were usually gay men of no fixed abode. He would often strangle the victims while they were asleep and sometimes drowned them in the bath. Dennis Nilsen's motive for murder was almost identical to Jeffrey Dahmer. Both of these notorious figures said that they killed because they didn't want the men they had met to leave them. They both, in their warped way, decided that being with a dead person was better than being alone.
Nilsen admitted that he used to talk to the corpses of his victims as if they were alive.

As a young man, Nilsen became obsessed with a painting called The Raft of the Medusa by the French Romantic painter and lithographer Théodore Géricault. The painting depicts the French naval ship Méduse as it arrived in Mauritania on July 5, 1816 after experiencing problems on it's journey leading to get damage to the Meduse as well as large numbers of casualties in the crew. What made Nilsen so disturbing was the way he came across as completely calm and highly articulate and thoughtful in interviews. If you met him you would have no idea that he was so dangerous. While many serial killers are reluctant to speak about their crimes or (ludicrously) maintain their innocence, Dennis Nilsen loved to talk about his murders and would discuss them for hours if given the chance. He seemed to crave attention.

Nilsen grew up in a small fishing port. He said it was a lonely existence. Nilsen had an obsession (a fetish one might say) with death. He saw a beautiful serenity and peace in death. This stemmed from a childhood experience when he saw his dead maternal grandfather Andrew Whyte. Nilsen said that looking at dead people also made him feel invulnerable. As a young man, Dennis Nilsen would smear himself with white makeup and talcum powder and pretend he was dead. He said he found this erotic. Nilsen deduced that he was gay at a young age. He said that this created a feeling of tension and alienation because he grew up at a time when being gay was still actually against the law.

Dennis Nilsen joined the Army Cadet Force when he was fourteen. He then served in the British Army Catering Corps and was a chef in 1st Battalion the Royal Fusiliers. Nilsen was stationed in Aldershot, Norway, Germany, Plymouth, the Shetland Islands, and the Middle East during his army career. Nilsen served eleven years in the army and reached the rank of corporal. It was in the army that Dennis Nilsen learned how to butcher meat. He would use this skill on his dead victims when he became a serial killer. In 1972, Dennis Nilsen moved to London to join the police. He completed his police training course and passed his exams. Nilsen had been posted to Wilsden Green Police Station and served as a beat bobby before he decided that this wasn't the career for him. When he was in the police, Dennis Nilsen had to view autopsied bodies in the morgue. He found this experience completely fascinating and sexually exciting.

Dennis Nilsen became a civil servant after he dropped out of the police. He was a recruitment interviewer. Nilsen, at the time of his arrest, was the Acting Executive Officer at the employment office on Denmark Street, Soho. In 1975, Dennis Nilsen began a relationship with a man named David Gallichan. They moved in together at Melrose Avenue and were happy at first. However, when Gallichan eventually decided to leave, this left Nilsen feeling lonely and abandoned. Nilsen claimed that he ordered Gallichan to leave. Whatever the truth, the fact that Nilsen was left all alone was devastating for his already fragile mental health. Old home movies of Dennis Nilsen and David Gallichan together suggest that Nilsen was the dominant personality in the relationship. One can see in them that Nilsen is an irritable man who likes to be in control of a situation. Nilsen always seems to be in a bad mood in these amateur films. Nilsen murdered someone for the first time eighteen months after David Gallichan moved out of the flat they shared.

Dennis Nilsen's first victim was Stephen Holmes. Stephen went missing in December 1978 and was only fourteen years-old. Stephen Holmes spent the night with Dennis Nilsen. Nilsen didn't want Stephen Holmes to leave and so strangled and drowned him. He washed the body (including the hair) and abused the corpse sexually. Dennis Nilsen's passion for necrophilia was the main motive for his murders. Nilsen said he was amazed to discover how easy it was to kill someone without anyone noticing. After he killed for the first time, Nilsen purchased an electric knife to dismember the victim but couldn't go through with it. He then began to see the beauty (from his point of view) in a dead body and decided to wash and keep the corpse. Dennis Nilsen would put plastic sheets or bin-liners on the floor before he dissected his victims. He said he would vomit in the sink a few times while he did this grisly task. Dennis Nilsen's murders are felt to have been spur of the moment because of his great difficulties in disposing of evidence. There wasn't much sign of any planning or thought about them.

When he lived at 195 Melrose Avenue, Dennis Nilsen had access to a garden out the back. He was able to dispose of some of victims by burning them on a bonfire. Nilsen had to throw some tyres onto the bonfire to mask the odour of burning flesh and organs. However, this never alerted any suspicion. One could hardly blame the neighbours. If you see someone having a bonfire the last thing you assume is that they are burning a dead body! Dennis Nilsen had to leave 195 Melrose Avenue because the landlord wanted to renovate the flat. When he moved to Cranley Gardens, Nilsen no longer had access to a garden and so disposing of the bodies became much more difficult. When he lived at 195 Melrose Avenue, Dennis Nilsen was a victim of burglars and two detectives came to the flat. Nilsen was amazed that the detectives didn't notice the foul odour seeped into his home from all the body parts.

Dennis Nilsen used a ligature to strangle his victims. Often it was a necktie. There were a few incidents of neighbours complaining of a smell coming from Nilsen's 195 Melrose Avenue flat. Nilsen told them that the odour stemmed from structural problems in the building. Nilsen sometimes put the torsos of victims in suitcases until he had a chance to burn them. The big cooking pot that Nilsen used to boil skulls, hands, and feet, was brought to his trial to be used as evidence. Dennis Nilsen's last flat was in a very grotty and squalid condition when he was arrested. It was absolutely filthy with plates and empty food containers piled up. The oven was covered in dirt and everything was old, tattered, rusted, and falling apart.

One of Dennis Nilsen's victims was a young man named Malcolm Barlow. Barlow suffered from epilepsy and had been found by Nilsen in the street looking unwell. Nilsen got him an ambulance and they parted. Tragically though, Barlow returned to Nilsen's building the next day and waited for him to get home from work. Nilsen found Barlow's presence an irritation and so he killed him. Graham Allen was Nilsen's second to last victim. Nilsen kept Allen's body in his bath for several days after he killed him. Nilsen would boil the heads of his victims and then pick off the flesh so he could try and flush it down the toilet.

Dennis Nilsen was captured because a plumbing company was called out to unblock the drain outside his building. Nilsen had been trying to flush body parts and bones down the toilet. Tests on the bones and remains blocking the drain found that they were human and the drainpipe led directly to Nilsen's flat. When the police searched Nilsen's flat they encountered a nightmarish scene. Nielsen had body parts and torsos hidden all over the place. He even had bags containing the heads of some of his victims. After he was arrested, Nielsen said to a police psychiatrist of his victims that - "They would sit down. I would talk incessantly like an auctioneer. Outpourings about music, politics, Margaret Thatcher etc. All completely cynical. If they entered into it, they would be OK. If they were sleeping, they would be dead already. It was the ultimate reply to apathy." This was a rather chilling statement because it implied that Nilsen would kill people who mildly irritated him.

Denis Nilsen wrote of his crimes - 'I did it all for me. Purely selfish. I worshipped the art and the act of death, over and over. It's as simple as that. Afterwards it was all sexual confusion, symbolism, honoring the "fallen." I was honoring myself. I hated the decay and the dissection. There was no sadistic pleasure in the killing. I killed them as I would like to be killed myself, enjoying the extremity of the death act itself. If I did it to myself I could only experience it once. If I did it to others, I could experience the death act over and over again.' Nilsen was sentenced to life imprisonment with a recommendation that he serve a minimum of 25 years.

Many felt that the Dennis Nilsen trial indicated that definitions of sanity and diminished responsibility needed to be looked at again. While it was true that Nilsen was aware of what he had done and seemed 'normal' in person it would be ludicrous all the same to call him sane given his crimes. This was a man who could make a cup of tea at the same time as he was boiling a human head on another hob ring. Nilsen was genuinely odd in that he wasn't insane but, all the same, didn't seem to comprehend that he had done grotesque and harrowing things. This is a man who would sit watching television with a corpse next to him.

Nilsen was moved around a number of prisons and even fought a (obviously doomed) battle to release an autobiography and music albums. Nilsen wrote tens of thousands of words in an attempt to self diagnose himself. The condensed version is that he was a misfit who found dead bodies attractive. Nilsen was interviewed for television once in prison but the interview only amounted to a few minutes as part of a documentary. In the interview Nilsen said that congealed blood made dissecting bodies less messy than it might appear. It seemed to be a source of irritation to Nilsen that he couldn't be interviewed more. His ego and vanity would have enjoyed more chances to appear to TV.

Dennis Nilsen killed all those men because he knew the connection he had with them was fleeting. He knew they would leave him and he didn't want that to happen. Nilsen once wrote - 'I had always held within me a fear of emotional rejection and failure. Nobody ever really got close to me. There was never a place for me in the scheme of things. My inner emotions could not be expressed, and this led me to the alternative of a retrograde and deepening imagination. I had become a living fantasy on a theme in dark endless dirges.' Nilsen's inability to cope with rejection became fused with a lifelong yearning for necrophilia. If he killed these men then they would never be able to leave him and he would also have complete control over them.

Nilsen could fufil his two greatest fantasies through murder. Until such time as decomposition took place that is. When this happened, Nilsen's necrophilia fantasies evaporated and gave way to more traditional serial killer headaches like having to get rid of bodies and body parts. You might suggest loneliness made Nilsen do these terrible things but that barely feels like a satisfactory answer. Most people feel lonely at times but they don't become Dennis Nilsen as a consequence. The most salient actor in Nilsen's crimes was necrophilia. Nilsen was addicted to the power he felt when he had mastery of a dead person. He was acting out his darkest fantasy. The fantasy could never be permanent though. The bodies would inevitably decay and smell. They had to be disposed of. Nilsen then had to kill again to begin the fantasy afresh. It was what you might describe as a classic example of a vicious circle.

Dennis Nilsen died in 2018 at the age of 72. He was at HMP Full Sutton in East Yorkshire when he fell ill. Dennis Nilsen died in York hospital. Nilsen died of a ruptured abdominal aortic aneurysm. It was widely reported that Dennis Nilsen was in great pain when he died because he refused to comply with medical treatment. After his death, a report at Hull Prison (where Nilsen spent his last months) said that Nilsen never talked to the staff and had no close friends or associates in prison.

The official verdict from the authorities was that Nilsen died of natural causes. When Dennis Nilsen died, it was reported in the media that the Ministry of Justice paid £3,300 for him to have a private funeral and cremation. Dennis Nilsen's ashes were given to his 'next of kin'. Not much much else is known other than that. It is not known if any relations of Nilsen accepted his ashes. There have been many instances where the family of a serial killer have refused to accept the ashes after the killer has died.

After his death, Dennis Nilsen's spectacles were given to a woman named Andrea Kubinova in the Czech Republic. Kubinova was Nilsen's penpal and visited him in prison. "He came across as a nice person," she said. "I know it's odd in the context, but yeah he was." Andrea Kubinova said that Dennis Nilsen told her he had no visitors in prison and that his surviving family had all disowned him. Andrea Kubinova said that when she met Dennis Nilsen in prison he was unrecognisable from the Dennis Nilsen of 1983. His hair was white and he was a rather hunched and frail figure.

There was a fresh wave of interest in Dennis Nilsen in 2020 when the ITV drama Des was broadcast. David Tennant played Nilsen in this miniseries. David Tennant said if Dennis Nilsen had been alive he probably would have gone to see him as part of research for the ITV drama Des. David Tennant said that in his research for Des he found Dennis Nilsen to be a boring person. It was true. Nilsen was genuinely dull in real life. It was only the grotesque things he did that made anyone interested in him. David Tennant said he was relieved that Dennis Nilsen died before the drama Des was broadcast because he believed Nilsen would probably have derived some pleasure at being the centre of attention again. It's hard to disagree with David Tennant's view that Nilsen would have enjoyed all the attention of featuring in an ITV drama.

Like many serial killers, Dennis Nilsen went to his grave with secrets. The story of Dennis Nilsen is one of the grimmest and most bizarre chapters in British criminal history. It is impossible to ever really explain how Dennis Nilsen came to be and why he did the things that he did. All we can say is that his strange fascination with death ultimately had tragic consequences. He was truly one of the most disturbing British serial killers of all time. He tends to be known as The Company Killer now because he never wanted his victims to leave him.

AMANDA PETERSON

Amanda Peterson was a child actress and eighties teen star. She was born in 1971 in Greeley, Colorado. Peterson made her stage debut at the age of seven. In 1982 she had an uncredited role in the Annie movie adaptation. She also appeared in the 1985 Joe Dante fantasy film Explorers. One of the child actors in Explorers was the doomed River Phoenix. In 1987 she starred in the comedy Can't Buy Me Love Love with Patrick Dempsey. This picture was a big hit and Amanda was put on the cover of all the teen magazines at the time as a consequence. Blonde and cute, a bright future seemed to be ahead of her. Amanda Peterson's last role in a theatrical film (that is to say one released in cinemas) was the 1989 movie Listen to Me.

Amanda was evidently not fufiled by her acting career in the end and seemed bored by the inevitable teen roles that were being offered to her. "Hollywood especially tries – well, I don't know if it tries to or not -- but it cliches these teenagers and it's really bothersome," said Amanda in 1988. "After a while every guy is trying to lose his virginity and every girl is whatever and, you know, they're like party animals." Amanda was said to be intelligent and fond of studying history away from the screen. She wasn't that bothered about fame at all. In fact, she could happily live without it. She got out of Hollywood as soon as she could.

Peterson graduated around this time and made an appearance in the TV show Doogie Howser, M.D. She would only appear in television movies from here on in. Amanda Peterson, at a tender age, was already what you might describe as a fading star. Her career had already peaked. Amanda quit acting in 1994 and was plagued by drug problems and trouble with the law. She also dropped out of college. Amanda got married twice and had two children. It was later revealed by her family that Amanda was raped when she was fifteen. This traumatic and awful experience was clearly something that deeply affected her.

Between October 2000 and May 2012, Peterson was arrested five times for various offenses including third-degree assault, harassment, DUI, and possession of drug paraphernalia and suspicion of distributing a Schedule 2 controlled substance. She spent some time in jail. For the last three years of her life, Peterson was receiving disability benefits and lived alone in an apartment in Greeley after her second divorce. She was found dead in 2015 at the age of 43. A report from the Weld county coroner in Colorado said substances found in Peterson's system following a post-mortem examination included the pain relief substance gabapentin, the anti-anxiety medication benzodiazepine, the anti-psychotic drug phenothiazine, and opiates and marijuana.

Amanda's family said she was in good spirits before she died and that this wasn't a suicide. They said too that she was clean and sober at the time of her death and it was simply an overdose of prescribed drugs. On his social media, Amanda's Can't Buy Me Love co-star Patrick Dempsey wrote - 'In my

memory, she will always be vibrant and young. Gone too soon. Sending my thoughts and prayers to Amanda's family.'
Amanda was cremated after a private service.

BRAD RENFRO

Brad Renfro was born on July the 25th, 1982, in Knoxville, Tennessee, to Angela Denise McCrory and Mark Renfro, a factory worker. He was discovered at age ten by director Joel Schumacher and was cast in the motion picture The Client, which starred Susan Sarandon and Tommy Lee Jones. He went on to star in films like Apt Pupil, Ghost World, and Sleepers. Renfro seemed like a vague cross between John Cusack and River Phoenix in his early days and looked set for a highly promising future. He wasn't a pretty boy and had a slightly rough and ready quality. He developed a big female fanbase at a young age. Renfro could be quite intense on the screen and this quality was highly prized by directors.

However, Renfro had demons that he never managed to get under control. Even as a small boy he was difficult to handle and had a knack for finding trouble. This was the case too when he grew-up. If he had been capable of staying on the straight and narrow and keeping out of trouble then Brad Renfro could potentially have been one of the most in demand actors in Hollywood. Sadly though this would never come to pass. Even before his premature death Renfro had already gone a long way towards torpedoing his own career.

In 1998, Renfro was arrested for cocaine possession and in 2000 he and a friend tried to steal a 45-foot yacht from Fort Lauderdale harbor. Renfro was pretty out of control by this point. He had further criminal charges for underage drinking and heroin possession. Renfro's once promising career began to stall and go into reverse. He was increasingly seen as trouble by the big studios and any chances of ever becoming a big mainstream star began to wane. If you are are a casting agent, director, or producer, you are probably not going to hire someone who seems to be permanently drunk and spends their spare time trying to steal yachts.

It has been speculated that Renfro was chewed up and spat out by the film industry because he was essentially treated like an adult even when he was still a minor. You could say that Renfro was another in the long line of blighted former child stars who went off wildly the rails when he got older. Not that being a former child actor necessarily means one is doomed. Look at former child actors like Natalie Portman and Ethan Hawke. They seemed perfectly sane and down to earth when they transitioned from child actors to grown-up parts.

Brad Renfro was found dead on January the 15th, 2008 in his Los Angeles apartment. He was 25 years old. On February the 8th, 2008, the Los Angeles County Coroner's office ruled that Renfro's death was accidental, attributing it to acute heroin/morphine intoxication. His body was taken home to Tennessee after his death. Renfro looked puffy and tired before his death. He looked older than his 25 years. In his last ever interview, Renfro had warned about the dangers of drugs and advised youngsters in Hollywood to stay away from the party scene and narcotics. The great tragedy of Brad Renfro is that he never took this advice himself.

NATASHA RICHARDSON

Natasha Richardson was born in London in 1963. She was the daughter of actress Vanessa Redgrave and director Tony Richardson. Natasha Richardsom was a highly acclaimed stage actress and also had many credits in film and television. She made her film debut as an uncredited child extra in the 1968 film The Charge of the Light Brigade. Her later credits included Gothic, A Month in the Country, Tales from the Crypt, The Parent Trap, and The Adventures of Sherlock Holmes. For her performance as Sally Bowles in the 1998 Broadway revival of Cabaret, she won the Tony Award for Best Performance by a Leading Actress in a Musical, the Drama

Desk Award for Outstanding Actress in a Musical and the Outer Critics Circle Award.

In March 2009, the 45 year-old Natasha Richardson was taking a ski lesson at the Mont Tremblant Resort, in Quebec. Richardson's second marriage was to the famous actor Liam Neeson and they had two sons and were blissfully happy. Sadly, the family was about to endure a most unexpected and sudden tragedy. Natasha Richardson fell on the ski slope while having a beginner's lesson but shrugged off the fall and said she felt fine. There was no sign that she was injured or affected by the fall. Most people fall from time to time if they ski and usually just get back back up. There was no warning that anything was wrong.

A few hours later though, Natasha Richardson began to complain about a bad headache and her condition suddenly became worrying. She started to become incoherent - as if she was losing the power of speech. Richardson was flown to Lenox Hill Hospital in New York City. It was very obvious by that something was seriously wrong. The actress was soon fighting for her life. It was a very shocking and perplexing turn of events because the fall had seemed fairly innocuous and Natasha was initially perfectly lucid and normal when she got back up again. There was evidently some sort of delayed effect with the injury though. It was only now that the full effect of the damage was beginning to manifest itself.

The accident had happened around noon. Richardson had tripped and banged her head on hard ice like snow. She didn't have a protective helmet on at the time - which was obviously foolish in hindsight. The ski instructor actually called for an ambulance after the fall but Richardson had refused medical attention and insisted she was alright. It could be that she was simply embarrassed by the fall and didn't want to dwell on it. Paramedics actually arrived at the ski resort at one point but they then left after being told that Natasha Richardson didn't feel she required medical attention. It could be that Natasha didn't want any fuss. She obviously had no idea yet that she'd been badly injured.

Liam Neeson was in Toronto making a film at the time. Natasha actually talked to him on the phone after her fall and seemed perfectly normal. She even made light of her accident to him. When her condition suddenly became serious, Neeson left his movie to be by his wife's side but they wouldn't let him in the hospital at first because they had no idea who he was. When he finally got to see his wife she was in a coma and had been declared brain dead. Her brain had been shunted to one side of the skull by the accident. There was no chance of recovery.

Natasha Richardson died two days after the accident. Liam Neeson approved the decision to end life support because he and his wife had made a pact that they would let one another peacefully pass away if they ever faced a grim situation like this. The New York City Medical Examiner's Office conducted an autopsy and ruled her death accidental, citing the cause as an epidural hematoma due to a blunt impact to the head. It was a shocking and devastating loss for her loved ones. One minute she was enjoying a ski lesson and then only hours later was fighting for her life after what seemed to be a fairly innocuous fall. Richardson's death was a sobering reminder of how serious any blow to the head can potentially be.

Natasha Richardson was laid to rest near her home in Upstate New York near the grave of her maternal grandmother Rachel Kempson. Ralph Fiennes, Alan Rickman, Laura Linney, Uma Thurman and Timothy Dalton were among the mourners at the funeral. Her last work had been a narration for the documentary film The Wildest Dream. This documentary was posthumously released in 2010.

In the aftermath of this tragedy there was conjecture over whether or not Natasha Richardson would have survived if she'd consented to the medical assistance which was initially offered. That is impossible to say with any degree of certainty. It could be that nothing could have been done. However, it does seem reasonable to speculate that if Natasha Richardson had been wearing a helmet that this may have mitigated some of the catastrophic damage done in this tragic accident. Sadly, it is all academic now anyway.

BORIS SAGAL

Boris Sagal was born in Ukraine (then part of the Soviet Union) in 1923. Sagal's family emigrated to the United States and, after an early attempt to become an actor, he eventually became a prolific television director (though he did direct a smattering of feature films too). Sagal was much in demand on television because he was competent, reliable, and efficient. If you need someone to helm a TV episode and deliver it on time time without spending too much money then Boris Sagal was your man.

His 1960s credits included Alfred Hitchcock Presents, The Twilight Zone, The Man from U.N.C.L.E., Dr Kildare, and Combat. In the 1970s, Sagal was equally busy and directed on Columbo, Ironside, and many other famous shows. Sagal also directed the 1976 TV movie Sherlock Holmes in New York with Roger Moore and the 1971 Charlton Heston movie The Omega Man. He was a dab hand with TV miniseries format too and earned four Emmy awards. Sagal was also the father of Katey Sagal - later famous for her role as Peg Bundy in the television comedy show Married... with Children.

Sagal's life ended in the most bizarre and gruesome way imaginable. In 1981, Sagal was hired to direct an NBC Cold War miniseries called World War III. The miniseries starred David Soul, Jeroen Krabbé, and Rock Hudson. It was a thriller about Cold War intrigue in Alaska. Arriving by helicopter back in Portland a few days into the shoot, Sagal turned and walked the wrong way after getting out of the chopper and was partially decapitated by the tail rotor blade. It was a gruesome and awful accident. One can only presume that Sagal was distracted or thinking about something else. Maybe he didn't have much experience of helicopters. It was just a terrible freak accident.

Sagal (who, amazingly, was still alive) was flown 60 miles to Emanuel Hospital in Portland, where he died after emergency surgery. He was 57 years-old. At the time of the accident, Sagal had been returning to his lodge after a day's shooting. He is believed to have spent about three days shooting background footage for the miniseries when the awful accident occurred. Sagal was survived by a wife and two sons and three daughters from a previous marriage.

They have an old saying in the entertainment industry that the show must go on and that was certainly the case on World War III. NBC replaced Sagal the day after his death with another director (David Greene) and started shooting on World War III again. Sagal's grisly helicopter death predated that of Vic Morrow in the Twilight Zone tragedy by two years.

ROD SERLING

Rod Serling was born in New York in 1924 and had a fairly extraordinary life until his premature death in 1975 from heart problems. He was a paratrooper in World War 2 and fought in New Guinea before taking part in the invasion of the Philippines (suffering bad shrapnel wounds in the process). After the war he enrolled in Antioch College in Yellow Springs where the liberal environment was an enduring influence on him and the motto was "Be ashamed to die until you have won some victory for humanity". Serling wrote furiously and eventually broke into television where he won acclaim for his dramas Requiem for a Heavyweight and Patterns.

He was briefly hailed as the new Arthur Miller, but became frustrated by the conservative nature of American television and felt constricted in his ability to address social issues. He discovered that it was perfectly possible to get scripts with controversial or political subtexts past the censors if one disguised them in a science fiction or fantasy setting. So was born The Twilight Zone, one of the most famous and influential programmes in television history.

The Twilight Zone, possibly the greatest television series ever made, ran from 1959 to 1964 for 156 episodes and remains an enduringly iconic part of American popular culture. It was created by Rod Serling - who also wrote many episodes and always presented an introduction monologue to camera ("Submitted for your perusal...") before ending each fantastical tale with a closing piece of narration in his distinctive voice. The series was alternately spine chilling and poignant as each week a variety of unsuspecting characters took a wrong turn into the Twilight Zone, a place where anything could and often did happen.

Serling wrote 99 out of the 156 episodes of The Twilight Zone but there were also memorable contributions from such names as Richard Matheson, Charles Beaumont, George Clayton Johnson and Earl Hamner. Serling was not the most subtle person to ever pick up a pen and always wore his heart on his sleeve but he was a master at the twist ending and conjured some fantastically imaginative stories for the series. Although he was always insecure about his own achievements it's safe to say they were considerable and timeless.

Night Gallery, which began in 1969, was Serling's return to fantasy television. The Twilight Zone ended in 1964 and he'd spent the intervening years writing several television dramas and films, presiding over his short-lived nonconformist Western show The Loner, and producing endless drafts of a screenplay for Planet of the Apes as he tortuously tried to work out a way to adapt Pierre Boulle's science fiction novel for the big screen. But Night Gallery would not prove to be a happy experience and failed to repeat the success of the iconic late fifties/early sixties phenomenon that made Serling famous. Night Gallery was so sour an experience that Serling even began to object to it being billed as Rod Serling's Night Gallery in promotional materials.

Although Night Gallery was Serling's concept and he wrote 35 out of the 98 episodes, he had no control over the production of the series and practically disowned the show. "On Twilight Zone I took the bows but I also took the brickbats, and properly, because when it was bad it was usually my fault," reflected Serling. "But when it was bad on Night Gallery I had nothing to do with it - yet my face was on it all the time!" It seems as if Serling did not want to have the day to day production duties of Twilight Zone and - as a consequence - found himself too far on the outside of Night Gallery. Whatever happy balance he was looking for did not materialize.

Serling felt the series was far too obsessed with the occult and horror when he had intended it to be a more eclectic fantasy show like The Twilight Zone. He was writing midlife crisis dramas like They're Tearing Down Tom Riley's Bar while the network wanted monsters and vampires. The fate of the series was sealed when NBC cut Night Gallery from an hour to 30 minutes in the third season and forced it to all but abandon the compendium structure.

Despite all the behind the scenes problems this series most certainly had its moments and remains endearing late night fun Guillermo del Toro has cited the show as a major influence on his work and Night Gallery (in the first two seasons anyway) had a very memorable psychedelic nightmare title sequence and fantastic spooky electronic music by Gil Mellé. It featured directors of the caliber of Steven Spielberg, John Badham, Jeannot Szwarc and Douglas Heyes and a slew of famous (or soon to be famous) faces. Diane Keaton, John Astin, Leslie Nielsen, Joan Crawford, Vincent Price, Sydney Pollack, Roddy McDowell, Zsa Zsa Gabor, Leonard Nimoy, Jon Saxon, Edward G Robinson, Yapphet Kotto, Larry Hagman, René Auberjonois, Richard Thomas, and many more.

Night Gallery could be bad (in particular, the short comic skits added to many episodes by producer, writer and director Jack Laird are absolutely dreadful for the most part) but at its best it was one of the great anthology shows. More than anything though it was the last consistent television showcase for Rod Serling's imagination. For that alone we should be very grateful that Night Gallery exists.

It's probably fair to say that Serling wasn't appreciated as much as he should have been when he was live. In the early seventies he brought in cash through voiceovers for documentaries and commercials. He did all sorts of stuff. He had plans to be involved in a film version of The Twilight Zone but sadly this would never happen. On May 3, 1975, Serling had a heart attack. He was mowing his lawn at the time. Two weeks later Serling had another heart attack. He was a heavy smoker for most of his life and not in the best of health. A decision was taken for Serling to have heart surgery but sadly he died on the operating table at the age of 50. It was a tragic loss for his family and a great shame for the rest of us too because we missed out on two or three more decades of Rod Serling scripts.

HAROLD SHIPMAN

Harold Shipman was born in Nottingham in 1946. Shipman was a GP in Manchester who murdered (at least) 218 of his patients with injections of diamorphine (heroin) from 1975 to 1998. He was known as Doctor Death in the British media when his shocking secret came to light. Shipman trained at the Leeds School of Medicine and became a qualified doctor in 1970. He was married with children and loved rugby. Harold Shipman seemed like the most normal person in the world. The chances of him one day becoming one of the most notorious serial killers in history must have seemed laughable at this stage of his life.

After working at a hospital, Shipman became a GP at a medical centre in Yorkshire. In 1975, Shipman was found to be addicted to a pain reliever called Pethidine (Demerol). He was forced to go to rehab for this addiction. Shipman then worked at the Donneybrook Medical Centre in Hyde, Manchester. Shipman appeared on the British documentary television show World in Action in 1982 talking about new treatments for the mentally ill - thus joining that select group of serial killers who appeared on television before their crimes came to light.

By the early 1990s, Shipman had three hundred patients at his practice and was a respected pillar of the local community. However, unknown to his patients and the community, Shipman was secretly killing his elderly patients by the dozen. Shipman first aroused suspicion in 1988 when a funeral home noted that he seemed to order a strangely high number of cremations. The police were called in but found no firm evidence of anything criminal or suspicious.

Shipman was caught in the end because he murdered an elderly woman who used to be the local Mayor. The woman's daughter was a lawyer and became very suspicious of Shipman. This suspicion was confirmed when she discovered that her late mother's will had been recently changed so that Shipman received the inheritance (which amounted to £386,000). The victim's daughter demanded that a medical examination of her late mother should take place to investigate evidence of foul play. The body was dug up and - sure enough - found to contain diamorphine. Dr Harold Shipman was naturally arrested.

People who knew Shipman were absolutely bewildered by the revelation he had been secretly killing his patients. They simply couldn't believe it. He was known by everyone to be a kind man who spent his spare time growing vegetables in his garden. No one had ever detected anything sinister or troubled about Harold Shipman at all. The body count is so high that we might never know just how many people Shipman killed. It is possible that Shipman's true kill count might be pushing 300.

And yet, Shipman never confessed to anything. He never admitted killing a patient (despite the overwhelming evidence against him) and never provided any explanation for why he had done these awful things. His wife stood by him too. Mrs Shipman maintained that her husband was innocent and stood by him during the trial. Harold Shipman was convicted in 2000 on fifteen counts of murder but hung himself (using bed sheets) in prison in 2004. He was 57 years-old. Shipman was reading Henry IV by Shakespeare in his cell when he committed suicide.

Shipman could not be buried for fear that his grave would be attacked. In the end he was secretly cremated with only his wife and children in attendance at the service. It remains a mystery why Harold Shipman did what he did but one theory pertains to the death of his mother from cancer when he was a boy. She required sedatives and regular medication. It is speculated that Shipman, who was clearly not the most mentally stable man, had an enduring obsession with putting people to 'rest' as had happened to his mother.

Another theory as regards the motivation of Shipman is (of course) financial. After Shipman was arrested, the police found that he had a large stash of jewelry he'd taken from victims and hidden in his garage. As a result of the Harold Shipman case, death certificate practices and the paperwork needed for a cremation in England were both reviewed and changed. The story of Harold Shipman remains very strange and unfathomable - not to mention very disturbing. True crime bios sometimes refer to him now as The Doctor Jekyll of Hyde. Harold Shipman truly was a bizarre and inexplicable killer.

PAUL WALKER

Paul Walker was born in Glendale, California, in 1973. Walker was a child actor in the 1980s and appeared in popular TV shows like Who's the Boss?, Charles in Charge, and Highway to Heaven. As he got older he began to pick up parts in movies - which included Pleasantville, She's All That, The Skulls, and

Joy Ride. Blond and handsome, Walker tended to gravitate (whether through choice or not) into action roles when he outgrew teen parts. He famously turned down a chance to be considered for the part of Superman though in 2003 when the comic book property was emerging from development hell.

Walker seemed to operate a step down from the A-list but this threatened to change thanks to the remarkable success of the car racing action Fast & the Furious franchise. Walker died during the production of Furious 7 in November 2013. It was a great shock to the Hollywood community and the world at large because, at the age of 40, Paul Walker was becoming a bigger star than ever at the time of the accident. Walker died in Los Angeles after the Porsche Carrera GT he was in crashed at a speed of more than 100mph and burst into flames.

Also in the car was Walker's financial advisor Roger Rodas. The car is believed to have left the sidewalk and then hit a tree and a lightpost. After the initial impact the car began to spin - whereupon it smashed into a tree and burst into flames. Drugs and alcohol played no part in the accident. It was simply a case of driving too fast and losing control of a vehicle. Walker suffered horrendous injuries in the crash and there was no chance of him surviving. Paul Walker was buried at the Forest Lawn Memorial Park Cemetery in the Hollywood Hills. There were two services, one for fans and one for family and friends.

After the accident, there were legal cases against Porsche by Walker's relatives due to the fact they believed that a defect in the car Walker was driving had caused the crash. Porsche were successful though in defending themselves against this lawsuit. There was speculation that Walker was 'drag racing' when he was killed but this seems to be a myth and there was certainly no evidence of that. An investigation into the crash cited the fact that Walker's tyres were pretty old and in need of changing. These tyres were probably a factor in this tragedy. It is of course darkly ironic that a man most famous for high octane car chase movies should die in these circumstances.

SHANE WARNE

Shane Warne was born in Upper Ferntree Gully, Victoria, Australia in 1969. Warne was arguably the greatest sportsman in the history of Australia - though Don Bradman would doubtless have an equally strong case. Warne was a cricketer who mastered the art of leg-spin. Leg-spin is a more difficult art than conventional off-spin and very few truly great leg-spinners have emerged because it is such a difficult skill to master. Warne by contrast though made it look easy. He had almost perfect control of a cricket ball and could not only keep the runs down but also skittle the opposition with unplayable deliveries. Warne was a once in a lifetime talent - the like of which we may never see again.

He was also a handy batsman down the order and so something of an all-rounder. The word 'great' is thrown around a little too loosely in sport but Shane Warne was truly one of the greatest cricketers ever to play the sport. Warne was an unmistakable figure with his bleached blond highlighted hair and earring. He was a bit portly and smoke and drank. He was something of a bad boy but mitigated this with a cheeky sense of humour. Warne was a huge presence on the field of play. He would 'sledge' opposition players, make exaggerated appeals to the umpire, and generally be up to all sorts of mischief. He hated to lose and was a fierce competitor.

Warne made 145 Test appearances, taking 708 wickets, and set the record for the most wickets taken by any bowler in Test cricket, a record he held until 2007. Warne was rated as one of the five greatest players of the 20th century by Wisden Cricketers' Almanack. Warne retired from all forms of cricket in 2013. He became a television personality, did commentary on matches, and set up his own charity organisation. He was an opinionated character who always said what was on his mind and this created a few controversies in the cricket world.

Warne was previously married with kids and had a few mild scandals involving texting other woman. He famously had a relationship with the actress Elizabeth Hurley at one point and this made Warne a big tabloid fixture for a time. In March, 2022, Warne was on holiday on the island Ko Samui, Thailand. He had experienced some chest pains during the trip and was planning to see a doctor. Though he could have no way of knowing it, those chest pains were actually an indicator that he was in big trouble and didn't have long to live.

Warne's health hadn't been that great as he suffered from asthma and had also endured two bouts of COVID. Those who knew Warne said he wasn't in the best of health because he smoked a lot and lived on pizza. He also drank too much - though his manager denied this. His manager said his hectic schedule and occasional periods of fasting to lose weight probably did Warne no favours either when it came to his health.

On March the 4th, Warne died of a heart attack in Ko Samui. He was only 52. It was a surreal shock to the world of cricket to learn of his death. People who knew Shane Warne just couldn't believe it. They couldn't process the thought that he was suddenly gone. 55,000 people attended Warne's memorial service at the Melbourne Cricket Ground. Many celebrities and cricket figures attended the service. One person who didn't attend was Elizabeth Hurley. She said she was simply too upset to go. Warne was laid to rest at Sorrento Cemetery in Victoria.

JACK WILD

Jack Wild shot to fame at the age of sixteen when he played the Artful Dodger in the 1968 musical film Oliver! Wild stole the film with his confident and charismatic performance as the cheeky Dodger. His Oscar nominated role in Oliver! led to Wild being cast as Jimmy in the NBC children's television series H.R. Pufnstuf. The television producers Sid & Marty Croft gave Jack Wild a lucrative 5-year $1 million dollar contract. To put that in perspective, adjusted for inflation, one million dollars in 1969 would equal several million dollars today.

Although they only made seventeen episodes of H.R. Pufnstuf, Wild was a millionaire by the age of eighteen and ferried around Hollywood in a Rolls-Royce for a blur of parties. He was a major teen heartthrob and star. In 1971 he was reunited with his Oliver! co-star Mark Lester for the cult film Melody and also reunited with another Oliver! co-star, in this case Ron Moody, on the film Flight of the Doves. Wild even recorded a few albums in the early seventies - although the sales were not fantastic. Jack Wild spent money like water as a teenager and young man. He thought this would all last forever.

Jack Wild's fame, like that of so many teen stars, proved to be fleeting. By his late teens he was an alcoholic and he found acting work increasingly hard to come by when he started to grow up and look a little older. Wild was especially frustrated by the fact that he was typecast as a cheeky kid/teenager - parts which he was naturally growing out of and would soon no longer be able to play anyway. No one wanted to cast him in serious roles. "When I first entered in the show business," he said, "of course I didn't mind playing younger roles. However it did bug me when I would be twenty-one being offered the role of a thirteen-year-old. I'm not saying I didn't enjoy playing these roles; I had barrels of fun, I just wanted more serious and dramatic roles; it's that simple."

Wild eventually married the actress Gaynor Jones (who left him 1985) and frittered what was left (which wasn't much) of his fortune away. He was also a diabetic and his heavy drinking led to three cardiac arrests. Wild even ended up having psychiatric treatment after spending the eighties in a booze induced haze. "I was taken to hospital and sectioned under the Mental Health Act. But when I came out of the hospital, I began drinking again. On a typical day I'd consume half a bottle of vodka and a couple bottles of wine. I'd sign on for Unemployment Benefit and use that for drink...at the same time I was expecting a phone call from Spielberg saying: 'I want you to be in my next movie!' It was insane."

Jack Wild looked prematurely old by now, his lifestyle taking a heavy toll on his once youthful looks. In 1989 he managed to get sober and was rewarded with a small part in Robin Hood: Prince of Thieves and some theatre work. However, in 2000 he was diagnosed with oral cancer (no doubt caused by years of heavy drinking and smoking) and had to have his tongue and larynx removed. Jack Wild died in 2006 at the age of 53. "I only wish I'd invested the money and not drank quite so much," he said, reflecting on his life, "but other than that I don't think there is much else I'd change. And I did have a lot of fun."

AILEEN WUORNOS

Aileen Wuornos was born in Rochester, Michigan, in 1956. Wuornos is arguably the most famous female serial killer thanks to a film and documentary which were made about her crimes. She killed seven men in total from 1989 to 1990. Wuornos had an abusive upbringing at the hands of a strict grandfather. Wuornos was a surprisingly beautiful child but a tough life obviously extracted a cruel toll on her looks in the end. She was homeless at fifteen and sold her body to survive. Tired of the cold, she eventually hitchhiked to Florida and married a rich man. The marriage only lasted days. He put a restraining order on her because Wournos would beat him up. Aileen Wuornos was a notoriously volatile person with an unpredictable (and rather frightening) temper.

After her marriage collapsed, Aileen Wuornos worked as a prostitute and, in desperate need of money, turned to murder. She picked up her victims on the I-75 highway. She would always target middle-aged men in nice cars. Wuornos would start to undress in the car and ask the driver to pull over somewhere secluded. Then she would get out of the car and shoot them before stealing their wallets. Aileen Wuornos would often shoot her victims multiple times.

Her alleged motivation for the murders was that she wanted to support her girlfriend and lover Ty. One might argue that a hatred of men was rather evident too. Psychologist Marissa Harrison concluded from her study that female serial killers were mostly motivated by material gain whereas male serial killers were mostly motivated by sexual urges. Aileen Wuornos was clearly motivated by her desperate desire to get quick money. Wuornos never really did much to hide the bodies of the victims. They were found fairly quickly and easily. A few men had a lucky escape from Aileen Wuornos. One man actually saw the gun in her purse and managed to drive away.

Aileen Wuornos was captured when the police finally managed to get an accurate artists impression of the killer. Once this sketch was circulated, they soon had a lot of calls telling them the illustration looked like Aileen Wuornos - an angry and violent local woman who seemed to spend most of her time drinking beer in biker bars. Wuornos was taken into custody and the police discovered that she had sold the belongings (like wristwatches and jewelry) of the victims in local pawn shops. Any money they had she of course kept for herself.

Aileen Wuornos claimed that she had killed the men in self-defence because they all tried to rape her. This was seen as a weak and improbable defence. It appeared unlikely that seven different men all tried to rape her at different times on the exact same stretch of highway. One of the victims was selling Bibles and another was a former police chief. They were ordinary people with no criminal history. The fact that Wuornos had not reported a single one of these incidents and always tried to hide the bodies also made her defence seem less than plausible.

Aileen Wuornos eventually pleaded guilty to five murders because she wanted the death penalty. She was tired of prison and court. Aileen Wuornos felt betrayed and alone in the end. Even her beloved girlfriend Ty secretly taped their phone conversations and testified against her. Wuornos became a born again Christian after her conviction. She always got offended when someone called her a serial killer. Aileen Wuornos claimed she was not a serial killer because she never tortured or mutilated her victims. While this was true she did shoot dead several innocent men!

Aileen Wuornos was executed in 2002. Wuornos declined a last meal before her execution and asked for black coffee. For $15 on crime collectible websites you can buy a photograph of Aileen Wuornos posing with a friend before her execution. She looks surprisingly happy in the photo considering the circumstances in which it was taken. Aileen Wuornos was a twist on the common serial killer situation in that she was a prostitute but a killer rather than a victim. She said she wasn't evil but just had a consuming hatred for the human race.

PAULA YATES

Paula Yates was born in Colwyn Bay, Conwy, Wales in 1959. She had a lonely and isolated childhood but in her teens found solace in the world of music and journalism. Yates met Bob Geldof, singer with The Boomtown Rats, in 1976 and they became a couple. Their first child Fifi was born in 1983. They were have two more children together - Peaches and Pixie. We've already covered what became of Peaches.

Before she became famous, Paula Yates posed naked for Penthouse. She was known for her short bleached blonde hair and was always considered to be quite a sexy sort of woman. She began writing music columns in her teens. In 1982 Paula Yates began her stint on The Tube - the show she is probably most famous for. The Tube was a live music show on Channel 4. It was sort of like a more obstreperous alternative version of Top of the Tops. Yates hosted this show with Jools Holland and it made her nationally famous.

Paula Yates and Bob Geldof got married in 1986 in Las Vegas. Simon Le Bon of Duran Duran was the best man. It is around 1985 that Paula first became aware of Michael Hutchence.

Hutchence was the lead singer of the Australian rock band INXS. The band appeared on The Tube in 1985 and Paula had to interview Hutchence. Paula Yates is said to have been smitten with Michael Hutchence at first sight and attended many INXS concerts simply so she could see him in the flesh.

In 1992, Paula Yates became a presenter on The Big Breakfast. This was a Channel 4 television breakfast show which was designed to be less stuffy and formal than the usual news based breakfast shows. Paula got the gig because Bob Geldof's production company was behind the show. Anyway, on the show Paula had a regular slot where she would interview celebrity guests as they lay on a bed together. If the guest was male you could usually rely on Paula to be a trifle suggestive and flirtatious. In 1994, Michael Hutchence was a guest on the show and interviewed by Paula. The flirting and innuendo was cranked up to eleven that day. For good reason too. Paula and Hutchence had already begun an affair.

The following year Paula left Bob Geldof and became pregnant by Michael Hutchence. Their daughter was born in 1996. Her name, in keeping with the Yates tradition of giving her children strange names, was Heavenly Hiraani Tiger Lily Hutchence. All was not well in private though despite the arrival of a child. Michael's friends later said that he planned to leave Paula around this time. Paula was doubtless frustrated by the fact that Michael had no interest in getting married.

There seemed to be friction between the couple and Bob Geldof too. There was the question of custody regarding Paula's other daughters. Paula was frustrated by the fact that Bob wouldn't let her other daughters stay in Australia with her and Michael for a time. Michael Hutchence is said to have loathed Bob Geldof and thought that Bob was a troublemaker. Whatever the actual reality, things were all a little fractious to say the least. Yates and Hutchence, as you might imagine, were like a magnet for the British tabloids and had little privacy anymore. They made headlines in late 1996 when they were arrested for having opium in their house.

Michael Hutchence was a troubled character by all accounts. He had drugs and booze battles and in 1992 had fractured his skull after an altercation with a taxi driver in Denmark. The injury left Hutchence with no sense of taste or smell and also prone to erratic behaviour and depression. In 1997, Michael went on a world anniversary tour with his band. Paula was supposed to go and visit Michael with her children in Australia during this tour but Bob Geldof took legal action to block that. On the morning of the 22nd of November 1997, Hutchence, aged 37, was found dead in Room 524 at the Ritz-Carlton hotel in Double Bay, Sydney.

The body of Michael Hutchence was found by a maid late in the morning. He had hung himself with a snakeskin belt. It later transpired that just before he died he had argued with Bob Geldof on the phone. Michael had obviously been trying to persuade Bob to allow Paula to take the kids to Australia. It is generally assumed that Hutchence killed himself because he couldn't bear the pain of being seperated from his daughter Tiger. Paula Yates had other ideas though. She said it was auto-erotic asphyxiation. Friends of Hutchence later said that he had been driven to the end of his tether by Paula Yates constantly threatening to kill herself.

Life was pretty tough for Paula after Michael's death. She faced a custody battle with his family over Tiger. There was also a bizarre revelation when it was revealed that her real father was the late television presenter Hughie Green of (the long-running talent show) Opportunity Knocks fame. On the 17th of September 2000, Paula was found dead in her London home from a heroin overdose. Friends of Paula said she had been happy at the time of her death and clean of drugs for two years. For some reason Paula had suddenly felt stressed enough to start using again. Her death was an overdose and not a suicide. Tiger was in the house at time.

Paula's memorial service took place in Faversham where she used to live with Bob Geldof. Bob arranged to have foster custody of Tiger so that she could be with her half-sisters. In

2007, Geldof adopted Tiger Lily and changed her surname to Geldof. Heavenly Hiraani Tiger Lily Hutchence Geldof is now 26 years-old and lives a fairly quiet life out of the spotlight. She was brought up in Britain but also has a home in Australia.

Lightning Source UK Ltd.
Milton Keynes UK
UKHW040644050922
408358UK00001B/65